Disaster Response and Homeland Security

DISASTER RESPONSE AND HOMELAND SECURITY

What Works, What Doesn't

James F. Miskel

PRAEGER SECURITY INTERNATIONAL
Westport, Connecticut • London

Library of Congress Cataloging-in-Publication Data

Miskel, James F., 1946–
    Disaster response and homeland security : what works, what doesn't / James F. Miskel.
      p. cm.
    Includes bibliographical references and index.
    ISBN 0–275–99211–X (alk. paper)
    1. Civil defense—United States.   2. Disaster relief—United States.   3. Emergency
management—United States.   4. United States—Defenses. I. Title.
    UA927.M55   2006
    363.34′80973–dc22   2006021374

British Library Cataloguing in Publication Data is available.

Library of Congress Catalog Card Number: 2006021374
ISBN: 0–275–99211–X

First published in 2006

Praeger Security International, 88 Post Road West, Westport, CT 06881
An imprint of Greenwood Publishing Group, Inc.
www.praeger.com

Printed in the United States of America

The paper used in this book complies with the
Permanent Paper Standard issued by the National
Information Standards Organization (Z39.48–1984).

10 9 8 7 6 5 4 3 2 1

I dedicate this book to my wife, Mary Ann, whose support and example have meant more to me than I can possibly say.

CONTENTS

PREFACE

Hurricane Katrina was, in some respects, a unique event for the United States. In terms of the damage it caused, Katrina was unprecedented. It flattened one of the nation's historic cities, killed almost 1,500 people, and dislocated hundreds of thousands of people in three states. The response of federal, state, and local governments to Katrina was also unprecedented in terms of the volume of amount of material and manpower that was mobilized as the storm approached the Gulf Coast and in the days immediately after it made landfall there. Despite the impressive steps that were taken, the response has been subjected to withering criticism for being too little, too late.

Unfortunately, this is not the first time that the government's response to a major disaster has been found wanting. There has, indeed, been a pattern of "failure" in meeting the needs of the victims of certain types of catastrophic disasters. It is critical that we understand the reasons for this pattern if we are to prevent another failure.

One of the courses that I taught while I was on the faculty of the Naval War College in Newport, Rhode Island, dealt with change in large, complex organizations. One of the points made in the course is that complex organizations sometimes fail for reasons other than the inexperience of or misjudgments by individual leaders. Often there are more basic, systemic causes of unsatisfactory performance.

In effect, sometimes there's just something in the water. And, if no one ever tests the water to see if something is there, the risk of another failure will not be diminished, no matter what other reforms are implemented.

There have been numerous examinations of the Federal Emergency Management Agency and the nation's disaster relief policies, but none have really tested the water. This is in large part because each examination has been focused on the response to a single disaster or terrorist event. That is to say, most of the studies have been "post mortem" critiques of the response to a Hurricane Andrew or a Hurricane Katrina—rather than a comparative analysis of the response to each of the major hurricanes for which the response was judged unsatisfactory by Congress, the media, or public opinion.

Further, most studies take too narrow a view of the elements that constitute disaster relief in the United States. Too many studies focus on the shortcomings of the Federal Emergency Management Agency, or indeed the shortcomings of particular people at the agency without fully considering the broader context in which FEMA must function—for example, the agency's necessary reliance on the response capabilities of other federal agencies, the agencies of state and local government, and private sector organizations. In fact, few studies look at disaster relief as a *system* that is built upon a network of interdependence among too-numerous organizations. That network usually functions reasonably well, but it has repeatedly stumbled over its own feet in certain types of major disasters.

Most studies make the obvious point that disaster relief would be delivered more effectively if all the involved organizations did a better job of preparing themselves for emergencies. Improvements could, of course, always be made in virtually every program, but the reality is that most organizations are reasonably well prepared for "ordinary" disasters—the thirty to fifty more floods, tornados, and moderate hurricanes that are eligible for federal disaster assistance each year. Where preparedness is lacking is in the realm of the out-of-the-ordinary disaster. Indeed, the frantic preparations that federal, state, and local government agencies typically pledge in the months immediately after a Hurricane Katrina or Andrew—before the press and Congress become absorbed elsewhere—only prove the point that the ordinary course is for these organizations to ascribe a low priority to preparing for the out-of-the-ordinary.

This book looks at disaster relief as a system—the same system that the nation relies upon to manage the humanitarian consequences of major terrorist attacks. It examines the system as it has evolved and functioned over time. A particular focus is the system's performance during Hurricane Agnes in 1972, the Three Mile Island near-disaster in 1979, Hurricane Hugo in 1989, Hurricane Andrew in 1992, and of course Hurricane Katrina in 2005. Each of these disasters has left its mark on the system, principally in the form of efforts to fine-tune the existing system while leaving its basic structure intact.

It seems clear that this fine-tuning has not made enough of a difference and there is no reason to believe that the answer is more fine-tuning.

Benjamin Franklin is supposed to have defined insanity as expecting a different result after doing the same thing over and over again. As this book attempts to demonstrate, this definition more or less describes our approach to reforming the disaster relief program. There is a depressing similarity to the recommendations that have been made in the *postmortems* of the major disasters covered in this book. I hope that readers will be convinced that the time has come to redesign the system along the lines I have proposed.

Chapter 1

DISASTER RESPONSE IN THE UNITED STATES: HOW THE SYSTEM IS *SUPPOSED* TO WORK

The disaster response program in the United States has evolved over time to include new features and capabilities without altering the basic structure that has been in place for a century. In fact, the program should be thought of not as a structure but as a *system* of programs. That is to say, it is a system in the sense that it consists of a number of independent elements that must work together to achieve common outcomes—such as the rapid alleviation of suffering by the victims of a natural disaster, industrial accident, or terrorist attack. The specific elements vary depending upon the location and nature of the disaster or terrorist incident, but fall into three general categories: the private sector (including individuals and both corporations and not-for-profit entities such as the Red Cross and the Salvation Army), state and local government agencies, and federal agencies (including the military). Private sector organizations, state and local government agencies, and federal agencies each have their own disaster relief programs and the challenge imbedded in the system is how to orchestrate these multiple programs effectively.

Although the focus of this book is on the federal element in the system, the reality is that after most disasters and even after most terrorist incidents, the federal piece is usually the least important part of the system. Except, that is, for the law enforcement aspects of terrorist incidents which are the responsibility of the Federal Bureau of Investigation and the intelligence community.

The response to most disasters is ordinarily handled and handled effectively by the private sector and local governments. Even when a disaster is large enough to warrant some federal action, the federal government's role is *usually* confined to reimbursing other responders for their disaster-related expenses after the fact. Federal reimbursement is ordinarily for the costs that states and communities incur in repairing storm damage to public infrastructure such as highways and bridges and to public schools, hospitals, and government guildings. The costs of clearing storm debris from roads may also be reimbursed. Families and individuals may also get federal financial assistance to offset losses to their homes and incomes due to a disaster-related interruption in their employment.

In a typical year there may be more than one hundred weather-related or other events that could be considered disasters—in less than half of those the state government would ordinarily solicit assistance from the federal government. For the sake of simplification, it will be assumed that this translates to fifty or sixty state requests a year for federal disaster assistance. The federal government would typically agree to provide assistance in perhaps forty-five or fifty. Since 1980 there have actually only been three years in which more than sixty disasters were judged to have been severe enough to warrant some form of federal assistance.

The policies for making the decisions about which disasters qualify for federal assistance will be discussed later but it can be noted here that federal assistance has been granted for some events that the average observer might not consider disastrous or even worthy of federal assistance. Examples include the authorization of federal disaster assistance in 1995 to compensate salmon fishermen for declining catches that were supposedly caused by unusual salmon migrations due to *El Nino* currents in the Pacific Ocean[1] and disaster assistance in 2000 to reimburse Maryland and the District of Columbia for the costs of snow removal. That the Maryland and District of Columbia cases were neither disasters nor true emergencies is evidenced by the fact that the snow storms occurred during the last week of January 2000, but the disaster assistance was not authorized until April 10, 2000—two and a half months after the snow had been removed.[2] In both cases the only "disaster" was that neither Maryland nor the District of Columbia had budgeted enough money for snow removal.

In the salmon industry and snow removal examples the "only" federal contribution to the disaster was financial. This has been true as well for the vast majority of the approved requests from the states. In all but a handful of instances, federal disaster relief amounts to a book-keeping exercise in which costs are shifted from the state's ledger to the federal government's and the federal action consists of little more than writing a check to the affected state and/or local government and subsequently auditing the expenditure. Thus for the typical disaster, the on-the-ground response action is really confined to two of the three system elements: the private sector and the state/local government agencies. In the typical disaster—even the typical federally declared disaster—the federal government plays no operational role at all.

It is a different story, of course, for the remaining handful of disasters in the average year that are severe enough to warrant the federal government to play a direct, operational role in the relief effort. Importantly, the federal government's plans for responding to the effects of a major terrorist attack on the United States are based heavily upon its operational plans for disaster response.

For the overall system to function properly after a truly major disaster or terrorist attack all three elements must contribute and in order for their contributions to achieve the goals of quickly reducing suffering and getting the affected communities back on their feet, timely and effective coordination is essential. Coordination is, of course, also valuable in less severe emergencies. But in lesser emergencies, the local or state authorities are individually responsible for making sure that all the pieces in the response puzzle fit together and that all the important needs of disaster victims are met. In recognition of this, the federal government has invested over the years in training and exercises that are designed to help prepare state and local officials to perform the coordination function. Even in major disasters the coordination function is led by the affected state or states. When a federal coordinator is appointed, his or her job is to orchestrate the response efforts of federal agencies, not to "take over" the entire response.

This book is about the overall system as it functions or fails to function in truly major disasters and catastrophic terrorist events. Although the focus is not on the after-the-fact federal reimbursement of state expenditures for the typical disaster, it will be argued that the federal government's continuing involvement in forty or fifty "minor" disasters each year may distract it from preparing effectively enough for catastrophic events. The book also offers an examination of the impact that the truly major disasters have had on the design of the system itself and on the policies applied by the federal government to disaster relief in general.

Despite the fact that the system functions effectively for the vast majority of disasters (although perhaps not always wisely—as when federal funding is authorized for minor disasters, as if the affected states really needed help), it is the perception of failure in responding to major disasters, in particular catastrophic hurricanes, that have resulted in the adoption of new, more expansive disaster relief policies on the part of the federal government. As the federal program expanded, the federal government acquired operational capabilities and preparedness responsibilities that are identical to what would be required for managing the humanitarian consequences of a terrorist incident and have, therefore, been incorporated into the government's anti-terror plans.

There are, of course, specialized capabilities for some types of terrorist incidents. Key among these special capabilities are protective suits to shield first responders from nerve gas, toxic fumes, and biological agents such as anthrax; decontamination equipment for radiation and chemical threats; and devices for rapidly identifying the specific chemicals or biological agents that might have been released by terrorists. Some of these capabilities exist only at the federal level—but many others have been imbedded into the state and local disaster response agencies. Moreover, the overall management structure through which these capabilities would be utilized to manage the consequences of a terrorist attack is the same management structure that is used in managing disaster response.

Given the widespread dissatisfaction with the system's response in 2005 after Hurricane Katrina, the subject of the federal government's disaster relief policies has again received considerable attention in political circles and in the media. Some observers have concluded that this particular storm was unique—that due to its severity and location, Hurricane Katrina would have stressed even a perfect disaster response system. Others argue that the shortfalls in the response were due to the fact that the people in charge of various response agencies did not perform effectively, either because they were not well prepared for the roles assigned to them, or because the program design or political considerations somehow prevented them from taking acting more effectively. A third argument is that the overall system is flawed and that until the overall system is redesigned, the response to major disasters will continue to come up short. This is more or less what the Senate Committee on Homeland Security and Governmental Affairs concluded in an April 2006 report. Oddly, however, the Committee contented itself with a recommendation that the basic structure of the disaster relief system be retained.[3] (The Committee's report and other post-Katrina appraisals will be discussed in more detail later.) There are elements of truth in each of the three assertions.

Hurricane Katrina was an unusually severe storm and its landfall happened to occur in the most vulnerable city in the United States—a city with a poor infrastructure, surrounded by water, yet situated below sea level in a region that is frequently buffeted by harsh weather. Moreover, the high levels of poverty among city residents necessarily meant that large numbers of people would likely be unable to take emergency precautions or evacuate without public transportation. These factors unquestionably presented challenges that no other disaster response efforts in our history have had to face.

On the other hand, the response to Katrina was not unique in that it was only the latest in a series of major hurricanes in which the overall system performed poorly. Curiously, the response effort after Katrina was also not unique with respect to the criticisms that were levied against the expertise and competence of the individuals in charge of the relief effort. Federal executives were, for example, sharply criticized for their failure to act decisively after both Hurricane Hugo in 1989 and Hurricane Andrew in 1992. Finally, it is true that some of the problems in Hurricanes Hugo, Andrew, and Katrina were, in fact, outgrowths of the program's basic design—but that design stems from the very structure of the U.S. government and is highly unlikely to change anytime soon.

DIVISION OF LABOR

As is the case with many federal-state programs (for example child support enforcement and welfare), the federal government is responsible for establishing broad disaster relief policies for all levels of government and for providing some funding and technical assistance to help build the emergency management capabilities of state and local government disaster agencies. Like other federal-state programs, the federal government is also responsible for the overall effectiveness of the disaster relief system. The states and local governments are, in turn, responsible for actually managing the response to the disasters or other emergencies that occur inside their borders. Unlike other federal-state programs, in disaster relief the federal government may be called upon to directly supplement the state/local operations with thousands of additional workers and huge quantities of equipment ranging from trucks and mobile homes to generators. Exactly what federal assets will be needed and how they should be used depends upon what the state and local governments understand their needs to be. As will be discussed in more detail later, this is a key, but fragile design feature. When the state lacks a clear picture of what the needs are, the federal manpower, supplies, and equipment will not be used effectively, people will suffer, and the recovery of the affected areas will be less rapid.

Whether the responsibility for the system's poor performance after ma-jor hurricanes is ultimately a state's for having failed to develop the necessary capability to both assess the situation and communicate with responders, or the federal government's for having failed to ensure that federal preparedness investments were used to develop those capabilities at the state level is to some extent an irrelevant question. The fact is that failure after major disasters is made more likely by the program's basic structure which fractionates responsibilities—not just between federal, state, and local governments, but also among different agencies at each of those levels. Another factor is that disaster relief is delivered in a political milieu which makes genuine before-the-fact accountability for preparedness at any level difficult and after-the-fact finger-pointing at scapegoats easy.

A fundamental underpinning to any examination of these arguments about the shortcomings of disaster relief is an understanding of how the system is supposed to work. Before turning to that topic, it should be noted that in some recent disasters there has actually been a fourth category of responders—foreign government agencies.

Receiving humanitarian assistance is not an entirely new phenomenon as some nations sent small amounts of financial aid after the San Francisco fire of 1906, but it is so far a rare occurrence for the U.S. government. Most citizens are undoubtedly much more used to thinking of American assistance to foreign disaster relief operations, after a cyclone in Bangladesh, famine in Ethiopia, or volcano in the Philippines, than to thinking about the implications of other countries sending aid here; but after both the September 11 terrorist attacks and Hurricane Katrina in 2005, some foreign governments did participate in the recovery effort. After Hurricane Katrina, the government of Mexico provided assistance in the form of military units who helped search for survivors in damaged Gulf Coast neighborhoods, and provided water treatment services and "meals on wheels" for evacuees. In what was perhaps a tongue-in-cheek gesture intended as much to embarrass the White House as to help the people of a neighboring country, Fidel Castro also offered to send 1,600 Cuban medical personnel to help treat hurricane victims in Louisiana and Mississippi. The Cuban offer was not taken seriously.[4]

Given the size of the U.S. economy and the strength of its governmental infrastructure, foreign assistance will never become an important element of the disaster relief system and will certainly pale in comparison to the roles of the private sector and state/local governments. While international aid to the United States will not be a significant factor in the overall response to domestic disasters, specialized assistance may be important in some scenarios. For example, foreign search and rescue teams could assist domestic teams in locating and extricating individuals trapped in buildings collapsed by an earthquake and foreign vaccines might be useful in a biological terrorism event. Finally, Mexican and Canadian assistance could also be significant in emergencies that occur near the southern or northern border.

THE FEDERAL ELEMENT

The federal Disaster Relief Act is the basic authority for the disaster relief system, but as has been noted, the Act essentially reflects the basic federal-state structure as established in the Constitution which leaves the primary *governmental* responsibility for disaster response to the states. Thus the Disaster Relief Act specifies that the federal government's role is to supplement the efforts of the states. This emphasis on the supplemental nature of the federal government's role has a number of practical effects.

One is that the federal government ordinarily would not get as directly involved in disaster response in a state as the state itself would. Another is that the federal government would become directly involved only after the state, in the person of the governor, has made an official request for federal action. Indeed, the Disaster Relief Act makes it clear that federal assistance—even post-facto reimbursement—is permissible only after the state has requested it. Thus to the extent that the federal government may have a direct role in a disaster response, it is by design a late arriver at the scene of natural disasters, although not terrorist attacks for which federal law enforcement agencies have a leading role.

On this point, both the media's coverage of disasters and the federal government's own public affairs campaigns have been somewhat misleading as they often imply that the federal government is one of the first responders. As well-intended as presidential visits to the disaster scene and meetings with disaster workers may be, the subliminal message to the public is that the federal government has a leading, perhaps *the* leading role in major disasters. A similar effect is inadvertently achieved when the state and local government workers who climb through the rubble of collapsed buildings are filmed wearing tee-shirts and hats with the logo of a federal agency. While it is true that these search and rescue teams are equipped and trained using federal funds, the workers themselves are usually from the fire department or emergency medical service of another city and, in any case, are not employees of the federal government's disaster relief agency.

Until 2003 the federal government's disaster relief agency was the Federal Emergency Management Agency (FEMA) and "FEMA" was the logo on the tee-shirts and hats that search and rescue teams often wore while being videotaped by the television networks for news broadcasts. In

2003 FEMA was merged into the Department of Homeland Security, but it has retained its identity as a distinct unit and indeed has continued to perform the same functions that it had in the past.

FEMA was established by President Carter in 1979, partly out of a desire to improve the efficiency of the disaster relief program and partly to alleviate concerns from the states that there were too many federal cooks in the disaster relief kitchen. Before 1979 three major and several smaller departments and agencies had responsibility for various aspects of the disaster program. The departments were the General Services Administration (the organization that builds or leases federal office buildings), the Department of Housing and Urban Development, and the Department of Defense.

Although disaster relief has since World War II been a civilian program and FEMA has always been (even under the Department of Homeland Security) a nonmilitary agency, many of the program's operational features can be traced back to a military regulation that was issued by the War Department during World War I. That regulation will be discussed in more detail in Chapter 3. At this point all that is necessary is to summarize its key operational features because they have basically been incorporated into the policy framework of the contemporary program. Those features are

State precedence. The 1917 regulation recognized that state and local governments have the primary responsibility for responding to disasters and that federal and military resources could supplement but not substitute for the state's efforts.

Federal certification. Under the terms of the 1917 regulation, federal assistance would not be made available until the federal government determined that the disaster was severe enough to have overwhelmed the state and local authorities. Although such decisions are made today at the White House based upon FEMA recommendations, the principle upon which the decisions are to be made is fundamentally the same as in 1917.

Federal coordinating officials. The War Department regulation designated the senior military official in the military district affected by the disaster as the on-scene federal coordinator. Today a senior civilian official is ordinarily designated as the Federal Coordinating Officer or Principal Federal Official to do roughly the same things that the designated military officer did under the 1917 regulation. Today, of course, the tasks are vastly more complex than they were when the War Department wrote its regulation. One measure of the increased complexity is the large number of federal departments and agencies that have disaster relief and terrorism-response responsibilities. Under the National Response Plan twenty-nine different federal departments and agencies may be involved in a major disaster relief effort.[5] Other layers of complexity have been added by the growth of the population and of the economy—both of which have led to home and office building construction in high risk areas—and the ubiquity of independent and competing broadcast and print media which increase the political pressures on the response leaders and also affect how the affected population behaves during and after a disaster.

Cooperation with local authorities. The 1917 regulation sensibly emphasized the importance of cooperation with local authorities. Obviously the same principle applies today. Contemporary cooperation with state and local officials has been institutionalized by the establishment of state and local emergency management agencies to work with FEMA and other federal agencies on an ongoing basis.

Accountability. The War Department regulation is proof that an unhealthy obsession with paperwork has deep roots in the history of the U.S. government. The 1917 regulation established detailed accounting procedures that required the senior military officials to keep track of relief expenditures, personnel costs, and other administrative expenses. The regulation even included model forms that the senior military official was to use. Today, a "finance/administration section" with similar responsibilities is part of every relief operation.[6] FEMA auditors also track expenditures after the response phase has ended and the overall expenditures are evaluated by the Government Accountability Office, an arm of Congress.

Avoidance of waste and abuse. The 1917 regulation required military officers to record the names and addresses of disaster relief recipients. In those precomputer days, the records had to be checked manually to prevent or identify double payments. The current disaster relief program has exactly the same goal of minimizing the issuance of duplicate payments, a hard thing to do when there are political and humanitarian pressures to distribute relief as quickly as possible. Indeed, Congressional auditors found that duplicate payments and other forms of fraud (for example, claiming storm damage on property that did not exist and overcharging FEMA for relief supplies) were not avoided during the response to Hurricane Katrina. According to a February 2006 report, there was "substantial" fraud in the program that FEMA administers to provide grants to individual disaster victims.[7]

Competition in contracting. The 1917 regulation also has a modern ring to it with respect to the rules it established for contracting with the private sector for food delivery, debris clearance, etc. The senior military official was supposed to ensure that written proposals were invited from the private sector and that the contracts were awarded to the lowest bidder. There was also a requirement that emergency supplies were to be purchased locally in order to promote the recovery of the local economy. Under today's guidelines, the general rules are similar even though it appears that they have not been scrupulously followed. Disaster relief contracts are supposed to be open for competitive bidding whenever possible—but a substantial number of contracts after Hurricane Katrina were awarded without competition.[8] Whether these no-bid contracts were appropriate or not, the basic principle that competition should be encouraged in order to keep costs down is the same as was in the 1917 regulation. In addition, the priniciples of the 1917 regulation have been reaffirmed in criticisms that the government did not award enough contracts to enterprises in and around the disaster zone after Hurricane Katrina.[9]

Equal treatment of minorities. There was no explicit prohibition in the 1917 regulation against discrimination in the distribution of disaster relief; but there was a requirement that aid was to be distributed directly to disaster victims whenever possible. This was a response to reports of discrimination in past disasters in which aid was given to local relief committees that were responsible for distributing it to disaster victims.[10] Federal antidiscrimination policy is crystal clear in today's program, even though there have been criticisms of the way that minorities have been treated during the responses to Hurricanes Katrina, Andrew, and Hugo.

As has been noted, in today's disaster relief program, the coordinating agency for disasters is FEMA and it is ordinarily a senior FEMA official who is designated as the on-scene coordinator. Presumably reflecting the judgment that practical experience is critical to the coordination function, the on-scene coordinator is typically, though not always, a career official, rather than a political appointee. In terrorist events the Department of Homeland Security may designate a coordinator from the law enforcement, intelligence, or disaster relief communities as coordinator. FEMA officials were the on-scene federal coordinators for the humanitarian aspects of the response to the September 11, 2001, terrorist attacks in New York and Washington, DC.

Coordination is one of those words that can have different meanings to different people. According to most dictionaries "coordinate" means harmonize various actions toward a common end—in the case of disaster relief and the response to terrorism, the actions that are being harmonized are the efforts that are being undertaken in each of the three elements of the system. It is the coordinator's responsibility to make sure that the actions are harmonized, but FEMA's and DHS's authorities and responsibilities are different in each element of the system. In each element coordination could be either proactive or reactive.

Coordination of before-the-disaster preparedness efforts, on the other hand, is rarely either proactive or consistently effective. Except in rare circumstances (such as the immediate aftermath of disaster when the images of the destruction and suffering are still vivid and the political pressures for action are still strong) preparedness measures have historically been regarded as a low priority relative to other government functions. As a result, the coordination of preparedness at the federal and state level has been only intermittently energetic.

The FEMA officials who are designated as on-scene coordinators in disasters or coordinators for managing the humanitarian response to a terrorist attack, according to the program's policy, are not representatives of FEMA, but rather representatives of the president. In theory this gives the coordinator substantial power to coordinate proactively, to direct other federal agencies. Indeed the federal agencies are bound to follow FCO orders except when those orders would conflict with their own statutory responsibilities. Conversely, in dealing with the state and local governments the federal coordinator has no directive authority and can only request or suggest actions by the state. With the private sector there is even less direct control and the federal coordinator can only encourage corporations, private relief organizations, and citizens to align their efforts with federal and state priorities.

The federal policy toward disaster relief and consequence management is documented in a National Response Plan that was issued in 2004.[11] The National Response Plan is itself derived from a Federal Response Plan that was issued in the 1990s and a series of predecessor plans that were developed in the 1980s for response to a catastrophic earthquake. All of these plans are remarkably similar in their basic structure.

Like its precursors, the National Response Plan addresses a central challenge for coordinating federal activities during disasters that has bedeviled the federal government since at least the 1970s. That challenge revolves around two enduring features of the federal government. One is that the federal response resources and disaster responsibilities have always been distributed among a large number of agencies. Under the National Response Plan there are twenty-nine different federal agencies that have disaster relief responsibilities. Some of these agencies have major subcomponents that are as big as entire agencies; for example, the Army, Marine Corps, Navy, and less so the Air Force (all part of one of the twenty-nine, the Defense Department) have each played important roles in disaster relief and have distinct organizational identities and cultures. The military's role will be examined more fully in Chapter 3. Here the point is that coordinating with the Defense Department during a disaster is not a simple one-on-one activity, as each of the services has different capabilities and availabilities that need to be taken into consideration in orchestrating disaster response.

There were twenty-five agencies with responsibilities under the 1987 Plan for Federal Response to a Catastrophic Earthquake.[12] The number of agencies has grown since 1987 as some agencies were removed from major departments and given independent status. There is an irony in this development for while bit players in disaster relief such as the Social Security Administration and the Agency for International Development have become independent, FEMA, which coordinates the overall program, has lost its independent status through its merger into the Homeland Security Department.

The National Response Plan attempts to deal with this organizational complexity by organizing the agencies into so-called emergency support functions, essentially interagency working groups of agencies with something to contribute to a particular disaster relief function. A lead agency is designated for each of the interagency work groups. However, this approach does not actually simplify the coordination problem very much, as the plan calls for fifteen different functional groupings to orchestrate the activities of the twenty-nine agencies. The number of functional groups and federal agencies that would actually be activated in a disaster response depends, of course, on the severity of the particular disaster, but it seems clear that any plan that involves so many groups and agencies puts too high a premium upon a commodity that is always in short supply: inspired and exceptional leadership. Indeed the federal elements in the system alone involve so many moving pieces that in a full activation of the National Response Plan, another layer of organizational structure is provided to *coordinate the coordination* that is taking place within the functional working groups. That other layer consists of the Homeland Security Operations Center and, for terrorist events, an Interagency Incident Management Group, both in Washington, DC.

The National Response Plan was the plan on the books in August 2005 when Hurricane Katrina struck New Orleans. The plan had been promulgated in December 2004 after a final draft and intial draft had been issued in June 2004 and September 2003 respectively. Thus the content of the plan should have been well understood by all parties by the time that Katrina struck. Moreover, the August 2005 National Response Plan and its two drafts reflected essentially the same operating principles and organizational design of earlier federal disaster plans. In fact, earlier versions of the Federal Response Plan took exactly the same approach to the problem of organizing the activities of the large number of participating agencies. The 1987 earthquake plan had eleven functional working groups and the 1992 Federal Response Plan which was the direct precursor to the National Response Plan had twelve.

ESFs	NRP	1992 Plan	1987 Plan
Transportation	X	X	X
Communications	X	X	X
Public Works and Engineering	X	X	X
Firefighting	X	X	X
Emergency Management	X	X	X
Mass Care and Housing	X	X	X
Resource Support	X	X	X
Public Health and Medical Services	X	X	X
Urban Search and Rescue	X	X	X
Oil and Hazardous Materials	X	X	X
Agriculture and Natural Resources	X	X	X
Energy	X	X	–
Public Safety and Security	X	–	–
Long-Term Recovery and Mitigation	X	–	–
External Affairs	X	–	–

Note: ESFs, emergency support functions; NRP, National Response Plan.

That such an obviously complex structure has been considered a necessary construct for two decades, three generations of master plans, and four presidential administrations (Reagan, Bush, Clinton, and Bush) demonstrates a remarkably consistent approach toward the problem of coordinating the many disaster preparedness and response activities of the federal government. Whether this consistency reflects inertia or the conscious judgment of successive leaders that the functional group structure was optimal is a matter of debate. It does, however, seem likely that the latter is not the case. A more likely explanation is that successive senior leaders realized that redesigning the structure of the plan would require extended effort and intense bureaucratic negotiations with all the twenty-nine agencies that had agreed to each other's roles as proscribed by the plan and thus decided to let sleeping dogs lie. Another factor is that each agency has powers and limitations that are prescribed by legislation and are reflected in the plan. Redesigning the plan would require passage of new legislation, which is itself time-consuming and might distract Congress from other legislative proposals that the White House regarded as higher priority.

The challenge that this functional approach seeks to overcome is how to work within the existing structures of government to coordinate the related activities of different federal agencies—agencies with varying capabilities, cultures, and ways of doing business that must work together in order for a disaster relief function to be performed effectively and efficiently at the federal level. The "Public Safety and Security" function offers a good example of the challenge. According to the National Response Plan, the public safety and security function is to make personnel and equipment available to a state to assist it in maintaining order during a disaster or terrorist event. The following organizations have a role in the function: the Departments of Justice, Homeland Security, Defense, Agriculture, Interior, Energy, and the Postal Service. Furthermore, several of these departments have substantial subcomponents with their own cultures, priorities, and ways of doing business. The Plan assumes that the coordination among subordinate organizations will be accomplished by the parent agencies. Thus, for example, the Department of Homeland Security theoretically coordinates the disaster relief contributions of its law enforcement related components (the Coast Guard, Immigration and Customs, the Border Patrol, the Transportation Security Administration, and the Secret Service) in addition to coordinating with the other departments in the group as well as with other functional groups. This obviously proved to be too much of a challenge during Hurricane Katrina and it is likely to remain a daunting management problem as long as the National Response Plan retains such a layered and complex design.

The second enduring feature of the federal structure is that only one of the twenty-nine agencies has disaster relief as its primary mission and that agency (FEMA) has always been small, dependent upon the cooperation of other agencies for success, and relatively powerless during the periods before disasters strike when plans and preparations must be made. There has been substantial commentary to the effect that FEMA's loss of independent agency status has enfeebled the agency and thereby contributed to the operational failure of the overall disaster response to Hurricane Katrina. Much of this commentary has been from former FEMA officials who were affiliated with a previous administration and have either an overly rosy view of the agency's status during their watch, political reasons for criticizing the Bush administration, or policy objections to the national emphasis on counterterrorism.[13]

As will be discussed in more detail, a review of the history of the disaster relief program indicates that the system has never responded well to major hurricanes. This suggests, of course, that the failure after Hurricane Katrina was the result of some things more fundamental than the bureaucratic status of FEMA and the skill of the individuals in the leadership positions of the numerous response agencies. More precisely, it suggests that improving the bureaucratic status of FEMA (or a successor agency) and adopting a more rigorous approach toward staffing the senior levels of the agency will not do enough to prevent another failure. Further, an objective examination of FEMA's history suggests that bureaucratic weakness is the rule rather than the exception for the agency. The record also indicates that the agency has often been staffed with executives who were not highly regarded in the field of disaster relief, but were instead apparently chosen for political reasons or because they were thought to be effective general-purpose managers. (FEMA is not unique in this regard as senior positions at other federal and state agencies are often filled by individuals who are not universally regarded as experts in a given field.) Indeed, the agency's "golden era" during the 1990s was more a function of the direct personal involvement of the president and vice president in disaster relief operations and the nature of the disasters that occurred during that time frame than it was of FEMA's status as an independent or Cabinet agency.

THE STATE AND LOCAL ELEMENT

The state and local governments have, as noted, the primary responsibility for disaster response and it is naturally up to each state and locality to decide how best to organize itself to deliver emergency services. Each state has chosen to adopt the same basic approach that the federal government has taken: a single, small coordinating agency that orchestrates the disaster response of numerous state and local agencies. Many states apply the same model at the town and county level, thus most municipalities and counties have a small unit in charge of coordinating local preparedness and disaster planning. Relief operations are organized according to the incident command system (ICS), usually under the direction of a senior official in the local fire or police department.

Most state emergency management agencies have, like FEMA, been merged into a larger department and do not have independent agency status. In fact, about half of the state emergency management agencies have been folded into the state National Guard structure. That is to say, the senior emergency management official in half the states is a military officer. There is no particular geographic pattern—states as diverse as Rhode Island, Tennessee, and Louisiana have adopted the National Guard model. There is precedent for this approach at the federal level. As will be discussed in Chapter 4, during the 1960s and 1970s one of the federal disaster relief agencies was organizationally part of the Defense Department. Canada's disaster relief agency has been part of the Department of National Defence since the mid-1990s.

The state emergency management agencies that are not part of the National Guard are either attached to the governor's office or part of the state department of public safety or another department. For example, the California Office of Emergency Services and the Georgia Emergency Management Agency are attached to the Governor's Office, and the Texas Division of Emergency Management is part of the State Department of Public Safety. The Florida Division of Emergency Management is part of the State Department of Community Affairs.

Like their federal counterpart, FEMA, the state emergency management agencies are typically coordinators rather than operators. In other words the state emergency management agencies typically do not directly provide care, shelter, and feeding to disaster victims; instead their mission is to orchestrate the efforts of the various departments and agencies with emergency response functions.

During an actual disaster or terrorist incident, the state government's role is primarily to support on-scene response officials who will, as noted above, be operating according to the principles of the ICS. The ICS evolved from policies adopted by the fire services during the 1970s in response to shortcomings that were identified in the response to wildfires in California. The ICS was since adapted for law enforcement and was incorporated in the plans for providing law enforcement support during the 1984 Los Angeles Olympics.[14] Since then, the ICS has been promoted by FEMA as a model for organizing during emergency operations and in 2005 the ICS was adopted nationally by the White House and Department of Homeland Security under the title "National Incident Management System." The ICS was used to manage the response in the Oklahoma City terrorist bombing in 1995 in which the chief of the Oklahoma City Fire Department assumed incident command. It was also used in the response in New York City after the September 11, 2001, attacks where the mayor assumed incident command from the City Fire Department.

According to a 2000 study, the following are examples of some of the coordination or management issues that arose during those California wildfires and that the ICS was designed to correct:

> Fire engines from the north part of the state would pass engines from the south on Interstate 5, each dispatched to fires hundreds of miles away when they could have been dispatched closer to home. Confusion reigned over the nomenclature for equipment, lack of compatibility of communication frequencies . . . and disparate command and span-of-control management approaches used by the dozens of responding agencies. At times even the most experienced firefighters were forced to throw up their hands in the spiraling chaos that crashed the public fire protection system in California during September of 1970. While there were plenty of examples of heroic and effective firefighting, these were accomplished mostly on a freelance or ad hoc basis.[15]

Readers who have followed the news coverage of Hurricane Katrina may recall that similar coordination issues continue to be observed in disaster relief operations. This, of course, suggests that the ICS has not proven to be a cure-all and that work still needs to be done in educating and training responders and agency executives about the ICS and building the communications interoperability that effective operations in any emergency situation require.

In major disasters, once the president has decided to authorize federal disaster relief, the state designates a state coordinating officer, frequently a senior official of the state emergency management agency to serve as the intermediary with the federal coordinating officer. The state coordinating officer is responsible for speaking on behalf of the state in terms of specifying the amount and types of assistance it needs from the federal government.

THE PRIVATE SECTOR ELEMENT

It is occasionally said, at least in the halls of government agencies, that in federal-state programs such as disaster relief, "the rubber meets the road" in the state and local governments. This is not strictly speaking true. The rubber meets the road in the families, businesses, and other organizations whose property is damaged in a disaster and whose members are injured or killed by the high winds, surging flood waters, or collapsing buildings that accompany disasters and terrorist incidents. Families and local businesses are also the first line of response in that they are the ones responsible for evacuating or for stockpiling the water, food, flashlights, and batteries for portable radios that they may need in riding out a storm and its aftermath. They are also the ones who board windows to protect the interior of buildings from rain and flying objects and who are responsible for buying insurance in the first place to offset the financial cost of post-storm repairs.

The Red Cross and other nonprofit, private sector organizations play a major role in disaster relief—indeed the Red Cross is actually assigned a major role under the National Response Plan described above. Under that plan, the Red Cross has the leadership role for one of the emergency support functions—mass care and housing. Even when the National Response Plan is not activated, the Red Cross operates shelters for disaster victims and helps feed victims and first responders. The Red Cross is not, of course, the only nonprofit, private organization that assists in disaster relief. Many of these private voluntary organizations (also known as nongovernmental organizations or NGOs) are church-affiliated and provide services such as feeding or providing counseling to disaster victims, helping disaster victims locate missing family members, and providing medical care.

Rather than list a sample of these organizations and describe their individual roles in disaster relief, it is enough for our purposes to note that the ranks of private voluntary organizations are filled with national, state, and local organizations and that collectively they contribute substantially to meeting the immediate needs of disaster victims. Indeed, there are so many such organizations that they have the equivalent of a trade association based in a suburb of Washington, DC, with more than thirty member organizations. The association is the National Voluntary Organizations Active in Disaster (NVOAD) which has been in existence since 1970 and which had a representative appointed to the FEMA advisory board in the 1990s. NVOAD is, like the Red Cross, a signatory to the National Response Plan.

For-profit corporations also play a critical role in disaster relief. Insurance companies, for example, often send extra teams of claims personnel to communities affected by disaster to expedite payments to insured disaster victims—clearly insurance payments can be far more important to a family's or business' recovery than modest grants from the federal or state governments. Insured losses from Hurricane Katrina in Louisiana alone are estimated at $25 billion. Disasters are, of course, expensive and can erase an insurance company's loss reserves and annual profit; but there is a small reinsurance market in which insurance companies in effect sell some of their policies to other companies or syndicates of private investors to share the risk.

One of the problems, as seen in Hurricane Katrina, is that many disaster victims do not have insurance; other problems are that not all insurance companies are as responsive as they should be and some insurance companies sometimes refuse to offer new policies in areas hit by disaster. For example, after Hurricane Andrew some insurance companies abandoned the South Florida market. These are serious issues that federal and state governments need to address, but they do not alter the fact that the actions of insurance companies in responding promptly to the needs of their policy holders in a disaster area can be an important part of the overall disaster response system.

Utility and telecommunications companies play an even more important role in disaster relief. Indeed one of the factors that determines whether a disaster relief operation succeeds or fails is the ability of a utility company to quickly restore power to the affected communities. Clearly, until electricity is restored, recovery cannot begin. Further, people who have remained in place during a disaster will—depending upon the weather conditions—grow increasingly uncomfortable and dissatisfied the longer their homes have no power. Health risks may also increase. Where residences and businesses use natural gas for heat or cooking, there may also be a risk of explosion or fire if service is not restored according to safety standards.

Power and telephone companies respond to disaster in much the same way that all of the other elements of the system do. When electric, heating, or telephone service is interrupted, the company decides if outside help will be needed to expedite restoration. Utility companies have standing agreements with utility companies in other service areas under which personnel and equipment are loaned to the affected company in order to assist in the restoration of service. For example, after Hurricane Andrew in 1992 repair crews came from utility companies as far from the disaster scene as North Carolina and Pennsylvania. Two hundred and fifty "imported" repair crews were on scene within twenty-seven hours of the hurricane's landfall. The damage to Florida Power and Light's infrastructure was so great, however, that about 350,000 homes were still without electricity four days later.

For-profit corporations like Florida Power and Light and Entergy New Orleans have obvious, selfish interests in restoring power to as many customers as quickly as possible. Indeed, the desire to recover costs and earn profits is what makes the free enterprise economy and the disaster relief system tick and has created a niche for for-profit corporations that actually help other firms plan for and recover from disasters. There are a number of such companies and the services they typically provide include arrangements for redundant records and data processing, stand-by operations and communications facilities that can be operated when the main facilities are damaged or flooded, and plans for keeping track of employees after disaster.[16] Disaster recovery firms have been in existence since at least the mid-1980s and contributed significantly to the quick recovery of their clients after disasters as far back as the Loma Prieta (California) earthquake and Hurricane Hugo in Charleston, South Carolina, both of which occurred in 1989.

THE SYSTEM OVERALL

Because the focus of this book is on the federal government's disaster relief/homeland security policies, the description of the system has been top-down, from the figurative highest level of the U.S. government to the lowest in the town or city level. As important as this perspective is, it is also instructive to look at the overall system from the perspective of a community affected by a disaster or terrorist incident.

When a disaster strikes or a terrorist act occurs, the first people on the scene are always the families, social networks, businesses, and other organizations in the affected community. The very first responders therefore are often family members, friends, and personal associates who help disaster victims move out of harm's way, give them a place to stay or offer them food and water, and contact local government emergency responders on their behalf to obtain whatever additional help may be needed.

The first element of government to deploy would be local officials, in all probability the fire department and police department. The first fire or police officer to arrive at the scene of the disaster would assume "incident command" under the ICS until he or she is relieved (as would quickly happen in a disaster of any size) by a more senior official from the local fire or police department.

Since the emergency medical services are usually part of the fire department, more often than not a senior fire department officer would in short course become the incident commander. As such, he or she would be responsible for orchestrating the local response, requesting help from neighboring communities, and, if even more help is needed, asking for assistance from the state. Once state assistance is authorized, the state emergency management agency would make the necessary arrangements, although in some emergencies a state emergency operation center might perform the actual function of directing state assets to the requesting community. In turn, the state emergency management agency or emergency operations center would determine what aid, if any, to request from other states and from the federal government. Actual requests for federal aid would, as was noted above, have to be first approved and signed by the governor. As assistance from other states and federal agencies arrives, it would be applied pursuant to the direction of the incident commander— thus theoretically ensuring that the actions of all local, state, and out-of-state responders are coordinated.

Private sector responses would occur simultaneously in the community and at the state level. Local churches and chapters of the Red Cross and other nonprofit organizations would gear up immediately on their own accord to provide shelter and food for disaster victims. Utility companies would begin the process of restoring power as soon as it was safe to send repair crews into the affected neighborhoods. Within a matter of days insurance companies would ordinarily be providing extra personnel to expedite service for damage claims.

This model, as described, applies to the relief effort in a single point disaster, such as a tornado or flood that affects a single township or city. The same model also applies to the relief effort after disasters or terrorist incidents that simultaneously affect several towns and cities, or for that matter all of the towns and cities in an entire state or geographic region. In these instances, there would be incident commanders in each municipality and a state-level incident command post (located ordinarily at the state emergency operations center) that would coordinate the allocation of response assets statewide and formulate requests for assistance from other states and the federal government. The federal government may also establish a Joint Field Office in or near the disaster zone where the federal coordinating officer and state coordinating officer—both with attending staffs—will colocate to coordinate the provision of federal assistance.

The response model obviously puts a high premium on capability at all three elements in the system and on effective coordination among the agencies and organizations at each level. This is both the system's strength and its weakness.

Chapter 2

WHEN THE SYSTEM FAILS

All natural disasters are, obviously, not created equal. Some are more powerful or geographically widespread than others and some affect highly developed sections of the country (cities like New Orleans) while others affect sparsely populated tracts. While the strength of a storm's winds or the height of a tidal wave can be scientifically measured, all of these measures fail to reflect the economic and social costs of a natural disaster. Importantly they also fail to reflect the "degree of difficulty" associated with providing disaster relief in certain disaster situations.

One of the points that will be made in this chapter is that the disaster relief system not only functions effectively after the run-of-the-mill disaster, such as a Category 3 hurricane or a river flood, it also functions effectively for *most* major disasters. In other words the system works reasonably well, if not always efficiently, when the degree of difficulty is within predicted limits; response officials know more or less what to expect from the event itself as well as from the other elements in the system; and they have planned and trained for the expected conditions. As will become clear, some storms—apparently only some *hurricanes*—present degrees of difficulty that most other disasters, even most other major disasters do not. This is not simply a function of the strength or power of the event itself.

Scientists measure the power of an earthquake in two ways: the Richter scale and the Mercalli Intensity Scale. The Richter scale is the more precise. It quantifies the amount of energy that the quake releases. The Mercalli scale reflects estimates of the level of damage that a tremor would cause in a given location. Naturally, the farther the location is from the epicenter of the earthquake the lower the Mercalli scale rating should be. The Mercalli ratings are subjective—the highest level, according to the U.S. Geological Survey, is "Damage total. Lines of sight and level are distorted. Objects thrown into the air."[1] According to the Mercalli scale, a strong earthquake in a small town in the desert could have the same intensity rating as an equally strong earthquake in San Francisco. Thus the scale does not address the value of whatever buildings and infrastructure would have been totally damaged, or the cost of repairing or replacing the objects that are "thrown into the air."

The Saffir–Simpson Hurricane Scale grades storms into the familiar five categories based on wind speed. Category 5 is reserved for hurricanes with wind speeds of 155 miles per hour or more. Obviously, higher wind speeds are more dangerous and destructive than lower wind speeds, but a storm with winds of 155 miles per hour is Category 5 whether it makes landfall or burns itself out at sea. Obviously, any storm that burns itself out at sea is basically harmless in terms of its economic and social effects.

With respect to floods and tsunamis, the height of the water is the key measure—wave height in the case of tsunamis and tidal waves, number of feet over "flood stage" for river or lake flooding. Here too, the economic and social effects of the high water depend heavily upon location. Floods over farmland may cause considerable loss to farmers and agribusinesses if livestock are drowned or unharvested crops are destroyed by standing water, but these losses will be minimal in comparison to the cost that would be incurred if the floodwaters covered a major urban area. The flooding in New Orleans after Hurricane Katrina is an example of the amount of damage that *some* floods can wreak.

The typical river flood naturally recedes as the crest of the water flow in the river continues downstream and drags much of the floodwater with it. However, considerable volumes of flood water may be left behind, trapped in standing pools that do not drain back into the river as the crest leaves. This is, for example, the case in North Dakota near Fargo where the slope of the Red River bank and surrounding land is flat and floodwaters can form shallow ponds or lakes that do not naturally recede. This was of course a particular issue in New Orleans after Hurricane Katrina when the standing water had no natural outlet because the city is below sea level.

For a flood, the levee breach in New Orleans after Hurricane Katrina was anomalous in that it occurred immediately after a major storm had dumped huge amounts of rain in a very short period of time directly upon the area that would then be flooded by a failure in the levee system. It was as if the Johnstown flood and Hurricane Agnes had occurred on the same day in the same place.

ECONOMIC COSTS

A more telling metric than the physical strength or duration of a natural disaster is the economic costs it imposes on the community or on the nation as a whole. However, as will be discussed, economic cost statistics do not tell the whole story.

Even minor storms have financial ramifications—from the cost a family incurs from a basement that gets flooded after a major snowfall melts, damage to shrubbery or crops from hail, and pleasure boats being battered by flying debris in heavy winds or sunk by high waves. Such costs are by and large private in that they are incurred by the affected families who obtain reimbursement from privately owned insurance, pay for the repairs and replacements out of their own pockets, or else live with the storm damage until such time as they can afford to fix it. Major disasters, of course, generate massive private costs as they not only affect a much larger number of people, but often result in significantly more serious damage to property. Major disasters also take a high toll on small businesses and large corporations. Businesses not only suffer property damage, but they also forfeit revenue when storms force them to close shop and interrupt shipments or when storms erode their customer base as a result of evacuation or lost family income. Major disasters also generate substantial public sector costs in the form of damage to government buildings, roads, and other aspects of infrastructure such as dams, canals, airports, and bridges.

According to the National Oceanographic and Atmospheric Administration (NOAA), the United States experienced sixty-two weather disasters from 1980 through 2004 that caused one billion or more in terms of damage.[2] Earthquakes, tsunamis, and volcanoes can, of course, cause considerable damage, but they are are not included in the list of sixty-two because they are not weather-related.

The NOAA report sensibly includes the value of insured and uninsured losses. That is to say, it includes losses for which businesses and individuals received private compensation as well as losses that were offset by government disaster relief programs and losses that were simply absorbed by the affected businesses and families. This is an important point for two reasons. One is that it is a reminder that private sector insurance companies (like utility companies) play an important role in the disaster relief system. After Hurricane Katrina, for example, insurance companies set up toll-free telephone centers to assist policyholders file claims and brought additional claims personnel to Louisiana, Alabama, and Mississippi from other parts of the country. Insurance companies also issued "quick loans" to policyholders to help them meet daily living expenses while their claims were being processed. The other reason is that it serves as a reminder that the absolute dollar value of the damage wreaked by a disaster is not necessarily a good predictor of the success or failure of the government's disaster relief operations. In all but a few of the billion-dollar disasters listed by NOAA, the disaster relief system functioned effectively.

Surprisingly, a fifth of the "billion dollar weather disasters" are not what one usually thinks of as disasters, at least in the sense of an urgent, short-duration emergency situation in which victims need immediate assistance of one form or another because they have been forced out of their homes and the normal utilities and government services have been cut off. As noted below, ten of the sixty-two-billion-dollar disasters involve droughts or heat waves that last for weeks if not months and which have such gradual effects that the "victims" are more likely to be crops and livestock than people. People have ample time during heat waves and droughts to take the necessary steps to keep relatively cool and ensure access to drinking water. In fact, for all their economic costs, droughts are not always even declared disasters by the president—they may instead be declared agricultural disasters by the Secretary of Agriculture who manages programs to reimburse farmers for crop losses. Whether they are "FEMA disasters" or "Department of Agriculture disasters" the point is that urgent care for people is not a factor, in the same sense that it is a factor after major hurricanes and earthquakes. During heat waves, bottled water and electric fans may need to be distributed to homebound individuals—but that is done by municipal workers and volunteers in a nonemergency environment. Another two of the billion-dollar disasters are for unusually cold weather in Florida. The 1985 "billion dollar" freeze was declared a disaster under the FEMA program while the 1983 freeze was declared a disaster under the Agriculture Department program. In both cases, the disaster relief consisted of after-the-fact reimbursement to farmers and food processors.

Billion-Dollar Weather Disasters:

20 hurricanes (including Hurricanes Katrina and Dennis in 2005)

14 floods

10 droughts/heat waves

9 severe storms

5 tornadoes

4 wild fires

2 crop freezes

Wild fires, of course, require immediate response and the response can be quite hazardous for the firefighting crews. However, putting out wildfires before they hit heavily populated areas is disaster prevention, not disaster relief, and on the occasions when the fires do engulf populated areas, the numbers of families and businesses affected are small in comparison to the numbers affected by hurricanes and floods. "FEMA disasters" were declared in early 2006 for wildfires in Oklahoma and Texas that affected populated areas.

Before Hurricane Katrina, the costliest hurricane was Hurricane Andrew in 1992 which rang up $27 billion in damages to South Florida. Hurricanes Charley ($15 billion) and Ivan ($14 billion) were the next most costly hurricanes in the United States. Both storms were in 2004. Hurricane Hugo in 1989 cost slightly less than Charley and Ivan, but the disaster relief effort for Hugo was not a success—as will be discussed there were factors other than the absolute value of damage that seemed to have determined the different outcomes for Charley, Ivan, and Hugo.

In addition to the sixty-plus billion dollar weather disasters since 1980 there have also been at least two earthquakes, one volcanic eruption, and two terrorist attacks that have generated costs of one billion or more.

The Mount St. Helens volcanic eruption in May 1980 was a spectacular event—one whose impact was felt in the form of ash deposits hundreds of miles away from the scene. Among the immediate effects were fifty-seven human deaths; massive losses of timber (according to the U.S. Geological Survey, the lost timber would have been enough to build 30,000 houses); fish and wildlife kills; damage to highways, bridges, and homes; crop losses and disruption to river and air traffic in the region. The estimated cost of these effects was $1.1 billion.[3]

In some respects, the Mount St. Helens eruption created the same kind of disaster relief scenario that heat waves, droughts, and some floods do. Just as downstream communities have advance warning that a crest of water is heading their way and communities affected by drought have weeks of advance warning in the form of rain-free days and unpromising weather forecasts, the State of Washington and residents in the vicinity of Mount St. Helens had considerable amounts of time to prepare for the disaster by evacuating homes on the mountainside (although some cabin owners refused to leave and some hikers either ignored or never received the eruption warnings). The eruption did not drive large numbers of people from their homes, nor did it necessitate the urgent distribution of relief supplies.

In fact, the federal government did not formally declare Mount St. Helens as a disaster in the State of Washington until three days after the eruption. A disaster was declared in Idaho on the fourth day after the event. This gap between the event and the federal declaration makes the point that as costly as the eruption was to the local economy, Mount St. Helens did not create the kind of urgent situation in which large numbers of people were injured or cut off from normal support systems. Further much of the costs associated with the eruption were in the form of lost crops (timber, wildlife, and fish in this case) and the expense of removing ash and debris.

The great Mississippi flood of 1993 is another example of a major disaster with multi-billion dollar costs. The floods were caused by extended periods of unusually heavy rain in the upper Midwest states during June and July, after an unusually wet spring thaw that left the ground saturated. Much of the $15 billion costs associated with the 1993 flood resulted from the cleanup of cities like Des Moines, Iowa. Some sections of Des Moines and other cities were under water for weeks. In addition to cleaning up the filth from the standing water, expensive repairs to municipal water systems were also necessary. Other major costs were associated with lost crops—fifteen million acres of farmland were flooded—and with repairs to levees and roads. As is always the case for downstream communities in a river flood, cities had ample warning that floodwater was approaching, thus the number of casualties was "only" fifty—a small number for a disaster that affected nine states and that caused flooding in seventy-five cities or towns.

Because of the dramatic effects of the floods on the economy of the heartland, President Clinton and Vice President Gore played direct roles in orchestrating federal disaster relief operations. Evidence of the president's and vice president's personal involvement in the federal response was the July 17, 1993, meeting they hosted in Missouri to discuss flood relief with seven members of his Cabinet, two senators, four members of Congress, and eight governors. The director of FEMA who was not a Cabinet member until 1996 (and lost Cabinet status at the end of the Clinton administration) was also participating as were the heads of the Small Business Administration and the Army Corps of Engineers. This direct involvement of the president and so many other senior leaders was very obviously a quantum leap over the ceremonial flyovers, photo opportunities with victims and relief workers at disaster scenes, and "rose garden" expressions of sympathy that presidents ordinarily confine themselves to after disasters. The nearest equivalent in terms of a president's direct engagement in relief operations was President Bush's involvement in the recovery after the September 11, 2001, terrorist attacks in New York City and Washington, DC.

Unlike floods, droughts, and hurricanes, earthquakes and terrorist attacks have occurred virtually without warning. Obviously the terrorist attacks on the World Trade Center in New York occurred literally and figuratively "out of the blue" and there had been no credible indications that the federal office building in Oklahoma City would be bombed by domestic terrorists on April 19,1995. After September 11, 2001, the Department of Homeland Security began to issue general nationwide "threat level" information and more specific alerts but neither type of alert has been specific enough to warrant the kind of steps (e.g., evacuations) that are taken upon river flood or hurricane landfall warnings. Examples of the "specific" Homeland Security warnings include the alert in October 2005 that the New York City transit system had a high risk of being attacked and the alert in 2004 of a possible terrorist attack on financial centers in New York City and Newark, New Jersey. Fortunately these alerts have not been followed by actual attacks and apart from accelerating intelligence efforts and increasing security on the buses and subways or around financial institutions, little was done in terms of preparing for managing the humanitarian consequences of an attack. The transit system continued to function and financial service industry employees continued to report for work during the alerts.

Warnings about earthquakes are analogous to the terrorist warnings in that they are neither specific nor certain enough to warrant evacuations or other immediate steps to reduce their consequences. In 1988 and 1989 the California Office of Emergency Services issued earthquake warnings for the San Francisco region. The warnings were issued in June 1988 and August 1989, but the "predicted" Loma Prieta earthquake did not occur until October 17, 1989.[4] The June 1988 warning was issued sixteen months before the actual event and the August 1989 warning two months before and whatever impact they may have had on the residents of the affected region must have dissipated by the date of the earthquake—as evidenced by the fact that a baseball World Series game was being played in San Francisco when the earthquake struck.

Warnings such as these and the typical terrorism alerts are thus unlike the certain warnings that precede droughts, heat waves, and some floods. Even hurricane warnings are more specific—initial hurricane predictions identify broad paths that quickly narrow and thus become more actionable for individual communities and state governments as the storm approaches. Indeed, those warnings have been acted upon by local officials who have responded by postponing or relocating major public events such as baseball and football games. Hurricane and flood warnings are also acted upon by individuals who voluntarily evacuate, or board their windows and stock up on water and batteries for flashlights and portable radios and by state and municipal governments who order evacuations, stop inbound traffic, and convert two-way highways into single direction (outbound) evacuation routes.

Similar measures could, theoretically, be taken if an earthquake was considered imminent in a particular area—but earthquake warnings are never that precise and the human and economic costs of false alarms can be quite high. There are, of course, general warnings about locations with a high probability of an earthquake that can and have lead to restrictions on building and earthquake-resistant building codes which over time can dramatically reduce earthquake damage—in much the same way that investments in building security (e.g., car-bomb barricades, shatterproof windows, particle detectors in HVAC systems) can reduce the effects of a terrorist attack.

The Loma Prieta earthquake in 1989 and the Northridge earthquake of 1994 were among the most costly disasters in recent American history—the Northridge earthquake alone caused $40 billion in damage—and the response effort was considerably more complex and demanding than the response required by most other large disasters—except, of course, catastrophic hurricanes. Because there were no actionable warnings—the kind of warnings that might cause people to evacuate the danger zone—the response effort to both earthquakes involved search and rescue in rubble and damaged buildings, treating the injured, and providing food and shelter to victims made homeless by the quake. After the Northridge earthquake tens of thousands of victims were temporarily housed in tent cities erected by the California National Guard in Los Angeles parks—eerily recalling the tent cities that housed victims of the 1906 San Francisco earthquake—but in this case the tent cities were taken down after a few weeks. Some municipal agencies in communities around Los Angeles also had to operate out of tents due to damage to their city halls. One reason why the tent cities were taken down after a few weeks was pressure from the residents who lived near the parks who did not want the parks to turn into semipermanent *favelas*. The fact that some victims of South Florida's Hurricane Andrew in 1992 were still living in FEMA trailers in 1995 must have been a disturbing precedent for the people who lived near the tent cities.

There are in addition to the tangible costs associated with search and rescue, distribution of relief supplies, provision of shelter, clearing and repairing roads and bridges, rebuilding structures, and replacing valuables, less tangible impacts of disasters. These less tangible impacts are hard to quantify, but are real nonetheless.

SOCIAL EFFECTS

It is clearly a fool's errand to try to assign a specific value to a life lost in a storm or to the psychological stress that would naturally affect a child who watched a parent being washed away by floodwaters or who saw the family home engulfed by fire. Nor should one even try to assign a value to irreplaceable items such as family photos, heirlooms, and other memorabilia lost in disasters. Every family knows that there are many such items that are far more valuable to them that what the insurance companies call replacement value. New photographs can always be taken, but they can never really replace pictures of deceased relatives for which there are no negatives. Nor can they really replace the baptism outfits, silverware, jewelry, furniture, and other keepsakes that had been handed down from generation to generation before being consumed in a disaster.

It is also impossible to put a price tag on the social costs of disasters. While it is true enough that the social costs of most disasters are either minimal or rapidly overcome by the restoration of "normalcy," it is also true that some disasters have lasting effects on the communities that extend beyond physical damage to buildings and infrastructure. This will very likely be the case for New Orleans and it was the effect in South Florida after Hurricane Andrew. Andrew displaced almost 250,000 residents, some of whom never returned to the area and the reconstruction resulted in an influx of laborers from outside the region. Many of these laborers were Hispanic and many chose to establish residence there and, in so doing, changed the demographics of the area.

Similarly, the population of New Orleans will never be the same in terms of numbers and perhaps in terms of its ethnic mix. Even the mayor has estimated that it will be 2010 before the city's population will reach 465,000 which was its level before Katrina struck. During this five-year period, many evacuees will inevitably find jobs and establish roots in other cities and will never return to New Orleans. Other estimates are that the city will never regain its pre-storm size. The pessimistic estimates seem more plausible.

A September 2005 survey of Hurricane Katrina evacuees in the Houston, Texas, area found that more than 40 percent of the evacuees intended to relocate permanently somewhere other than New Orleans. These were mostly long-time New Orleans residents—90 percent of them had lived in the city for at least ten years; 75 percent told interviewers they had lived in New Orleans their entire lives, up to their evacuation.[5] Lending credence to this finding is the study methodology which involved in-person interviews of the evacuees by professional interviewers, rather than brief telephone surveys by amatuer interviewers.

It is certainly possible that the Houston evacuees are not representative of the entire population of evacuees, although the Houston area has a larger number of Katrina evacuees than any other metropolitan area. As of the end of October 2005—after the Houston survey—there were about 300,000 evacuees in the greater Houston area.[6] Although many of the 300,000 were evacuated from areas other than New Orleans, the September 2005 survey involved only evacuees from the city.

Indeed, an October 2005 telephone survey of evacuees nationwide by USA Today, CNN, and the Gallup organization did find a smaller percentage "nonreturners." However the smaller percentage was still substantial—20 percent of the respondents said they did not intend to return to New Orleans and planned on establishing new homes elsewhere.[7] It is not clear what proportion of these respondents had actually been long-time residents of New Orleans, but even if the proportion of nonreturning residents is closer to 20 percent than 40 percent the effect on the city will be dramatic. Finally, a National Science Foundation report in January 2006 predicted that as much as 80 percent of the city's African-American population would not return to the city—due to the extent of damage in their neighborhoods many would have no homes to return to for a year or more and others would have settled elsewhere by the time their former neighborhoods were rehabilitated.[8]

It appears that the loss of the nonreturning evacuee population will be partly offset by an increase in the city's Hispanic population. Prior to Hurricane Katrina, New Orleans' population was predominately African-American with a very small Hispanic population. According to the 2000 census, about two-thirds of the city's population was African-American, a little less than three-tenths was white, 3 percent was Hispanic and 2 percent was Asian.[9] Media reports about the reconstruction effort in the city indicate that a substantial number of workers in the construction and affiliated trades are Hispanic and it is widely expected that a significant number of them will remain in New Orleans for an extended period of time—in effect, replacing many of the nonreturning evacuees. The result will be a shift in the demographics of the city as the proportion of Hispanics increases and the proportion of African-Americans decreases.

For example, *Newsweek* reported in December 2005 that there were substantial numbers of laborers with Central American roots in the recovery work force and that at an October 2005 conference with business leaders, the mayor had expressed concern about the size of the influx of Hispanic workers.[10] (The mayor's remarks were subsequently recanted after being denounced by the U.S. Hispanic Chamber of Commerce which pointed with justifiable pride to the contribution that the Hispanic workers were making to the city's recovery.[11]) The New Orleans *Times-Picayune* observed in October 2005 and January 2006 that the city's reconstruction effort depended heavily on Hispanic laborers who had moved to the city for jobs.[12]

It is important to dismiss any implication that the demographic effects of Hurricane Katrina are inherently negative. They are in some respects positive. For example, many of the evacuees who do not return to New Orleans presumably will chose not to do so because they have little to return to. Or, because they have found better jobs or educational opportunities in the areas to which they evacuated. Further, the Hispanic and other workers who migrate to New Orleans for jobs and decide to stay in the city presumably would only do so because they are better off in New Orleans than they were in their previous domiciles.

Moreover, while the city itself will have a different character after reconstruction is complete—setting aside the question of whether the city should have been rebuilt in the same exposed location in the first place—it is fair to say that a different demographic character is neither good nor bad. It is only different. It is also fair to say that pre-Katrina New Orleans was in any case in desperate need of a makeover. According to 2000 census data, the city had a poverty rate that was almost three times as high as that of the rest of the country.[13] Its school system has chronically underperformed and many of its school buildings were old and dilapidated. The reconstruction could result in an infrastructure that is better than the ante-Katrina infrastructure and a smaller population might also reduce the strain on the city's new infrastructure.

There is one social effect of the storm that is undeniably negative—an increase in racial tensions. Opinion polls indicate that a high proportion of African-Americans believe that the nation and its government would have responded more effectively if New Orleans had had a predominately white population. Whether the resentments that result from this feeling have any lasting effects obviously remains to be seen; but claims by some African-American opinion leaders that there were "racist" motives behind the government's action and inaction undoubtedly help to keep the embers of resentment burning.

DEGREE OF DIFFICULTY

For the vast majority of disasters, the system functions effectively but there have been periodic failures. The lessons drawn (if not actually *learned* in sense of having been permanently assimilated by the bureaucracy at the federal, state/local, and private sector levels) from these periodic failures have led to major adjustments in federal disaster relief policies and budgets—but not in the basic framework of the system.

A useful starting point for an examination of the types of disasters in which systemic failures have occurred is to review the definition of the term disaster. According to the Robert T. Stafford Disaster Relief and Emergency Assistance Act (as amended on 2000), a major disaster is

> any natural catastrophe (including any hurricane, tornado, storm, high water, wind driven water, tidal wave, tsunami, earthquake, volcanic eruption, landslide, mudslide, snowstorm, or drought), or, regardless of cause, any fire, flood, or explosion, in any part of the United States, which in the

determination of the President causes damage of sufficient severity and magnitude to warrant major disaster assistance under this Act to supplement the efforts and available resources of States, local governments, and disaster relief organizations in alleviating the damage, loss, hardship, or suffering caused thereby.[14]

Importantly, disasters that strike densely populated or industrially developed sections of the United States are never "just" hurricanes, floods, or earthquakes and terrorist attacks in those areas are never "just" criminal violence. Each of these events are often accompanied by fires, explosions, dangerous levels of pollution, and other developments that compound the effects on the population, sharply increase the amount of damage, and complicate the response effort. For example, much of the damage caused by the 1906 earthquake in San Francisco resulted from the fires that swept the city after the ground stopped shaking. Since 1906 there have been such dramatic improvements in municipal building codes, the robustness of public water systems, and the response capabilities of fire departments and utility companies that the Loma Prieta and Northridge earthquakes—both of which took place in fairly densely populated and developed areas—were not followed by widespread fire. The fires that did break out in the Marina district of San Francisco after the Loma Prieta earthquake were contained and quickly extinguished.

It is only when the disaster is found to be "major" that federal assistance is supposed to be made available. As has been noted, there have been instances in which the lower end of the spectrum of what constitutes a "major" disaster seems to have been somewhat blurred in practice—but our focus here is on the upper end of the spectrum where there is no doubt that the adjective "major" applies and the demand for an effective response by the disaster relief system is great.

The Disaster Relief and Emergency Assistance Act also allows for federal assistance in "emergencies" to supplement the efforts of state and local governments when the president determines such assistance is needed to save lives, avert a catastrophe, or protect property and public health. Typically, emergency declarations are more limited in nature than a disaster declaration and are for specific forms of reimbursement to state and local governments, for example to defray the costs incurred by the states of Louisiana and Texas in conducting searches for debris from the *Columbia* space shuttle explosion in 2003. There were sixty-eight emergency declarations in 2005, an unusually high number. The average annual total of emergency declarations for the preceding five years was less than nine. The figure for 2005 was the direct result of Hurricane Katrina. Forty-eight of the emergency declarations in 2005 were necessary to authorize federal assistance to the states that were taking in Katrina evacuees and thus could properly be thought of as part of the disaster relief operation, not as a separate emergency.

The disaster relief legislation does not specify standards for evaluating the success or failure of disaster relief operations, nor has FEMA or any other federal entity articulated objective criteria against which disaster operations should be judged. Thus, judgments about whether a particular disaster relief operation has been a success or failure are necessarily subjective.

However, judging from the political criticism that has been levied against the response to Hurricane Katrina, some standards can be inferred. The following are the key standards of a successful disaster relief operation:

Claims for federal disaster assistance payments are processed rapidly and applicants are not forced to wait extended periods of time to apply for disaster assistance.

Few if any disaster victims remain stranded in life-threatening situations or without urgent medical attention for more than a few hours.

Few if any disaster victims are left without adequate shelter, food, or water for more than twenty-four hours.

Individuals seeking to evacuate are able to do so.

Electricity, water, and communications utilities are restored to the vast majority of the people in the affected area within twenty-four or thirty-six hours.

If these implicit standards are reasonable, two questions arise. One is the extent to which these standards have been met by the disaster response system. The answer to this question is undeniable: for most disasters, the standards have been met. This suggests that the most interesting question is the second: do some disasters simply present situations in which the "degree of difficulty" for the disaster response system is simply too high and, if so, what features of the disaster situation contribute most to the problem?

"Degree of difficulty" is a term that has been borrowed from the Olympics, in particular Olympic figure skating and diving. Each skating routine and dive is categorized according to its complexity, physical demand, and risk of failure. Judges accord higher scores to the successful execution of routines with high degrees of difficulty, than to success at routines with low degrees of difficulty.

Much the same must be said about disaster relief operations—some are simply easier than others to execute. Even some of the costliest disasters in the nation's history have had relatively low degrees of difficulty. As noted above, response operations are obviously less difficult when there has been actionable warning for people, local businesses, and governments and when that warning has actually been acted upon. Response operations are also less difficult when the principal operation is reimbursement for losses. If there is one thing that the federal government does well under any and all conditions, it is writing checks.

The second question is what features of disaster situation contribute most to a high degree of difficulty in rapidly processing disaster relief claims; rescuing victims whose lives are threatened; providing adequate shelter, food, and medical care; enabling evacuations; and restoring electric, water, and communications services. As will be seen, there are indeed common "high degree of difficulty" features in the three disaster relief operations that have been most heavily criticized: hurricanes Hugo, Andrew, and Katrina. The responses to these disasters will be examined in more detail in Chapter 5 and Chapter 6 and conclusions about the design of the disaster relief program and recommendations for change in the future will be addressed in Chapter 7 and Chapter 8. Before then, however, we will briefly review the role of the military in disaster operations and the history of the FEMA.

In concluding this chapter, several observations are warranted. One is that the physical strength of a weather disaster, a geologic event such as an earthquake, or even a terrorist bomb tells less than half the disaster relief story. A more useful measure is the economic cost that the storm or event imposes upon society; but even then important social effects would be omitted. A second observation is an obvious one, size and location do matter. All other things being equal, disasters that span large geographic areas tend to have a higher degree of difficulty, both because their victims are widely distributed and because they involve multiple state and/or local jurisdictions.

In fact, one of the most important factors in determining both the degree of difficulty of a relief operation and the cost of the disaster itself is the ability of the state and municipal governments to collect and accurately interpret information about the disaster situation as it unfolds—arguably more difficult when large areas are affected, as well as the ability of municipal governments and utility companies to contain the secondary effects of a disaster. Secondary effects include fires, toxic spills, and industrial explosions that often occur when disasters strike. Fortunately this is less of a problem than in the past as municipal fire departments are much more capable of containing fires than they were in the era of the Chicago fire of 1871 and the San Francisco earthquake of 1906. Additionally, the regulated utility companies now generally do an excellent job of rapidly shutting gas lines to prevent fires and ensuring safe restoration of natural gas service to homes and businesses afterwards. Improvements in building materials (concrete and steel, instead of wood, fire-retardant carpets, and insulation) and in the application of fire safety regulations (sprinklers in public buildings, smoke detection systems in private homes) also help inhibit the spread of fires in at least the newer sections of American cities.

A third observation is that given the inherent complexity of the disaster relief system with its numerous moving parts at each of the federal, state/local, and private sector levels, some degree of difficulty is virtually hardwired into the system. Any system in which nearly thirty federal agencies, most with distinct subagency components, play separate roles is by definition complex. Further, the complexity at the federal level is more than replicated at the state level where numerous state agencies, public utility commissions, and county and municipal agencies and elected officials may be involved. Then there are responders in the private sector such as the Red Cross, the Salvation Army, local churches, corporations, utility companies—and not just from the states directly affected by the disaster. Out-of-state corporations and voluntary organizations also lend their hands to the relief operations, as do National Guard and civilian agencies from states not directly affected by the disaster. Despite its complexity, the system can and does work, but the history of disasters shows that under certain conditions coordination (what the military calls "unity of effort") among the various entities responsible for providing disaster relief does not flow as scripted and must be forced.

That is why a federal coordinating official is designated as the president's on-scene representative during major disasters, although FEMA designees evidently do not always act as if they are as empowered as the system design appears to envision. That is also why, as we shall see, special envoys—a domestic equivalent of a plenipotentiary sent overseas with full power to negotiate a treaty—have on some occasions been necessary. Specially empowered officials were sent to take charge of the response after Hurricanes Agnes, Andrew, and Katrina. President Clinton's flood relief summit in Missouri is another example where extraordinary steps were taken to achieve unity of effort.

Chapter 3

DISASTER RELIEF AND THE MILITARY: CIVIL DEFENSE AND HOMELAND SECURITY

The armed forces have played important roles in disaster relief since the very beginning of the republic, and military involvement in disasters is hardly unique to the United States. In fact, military involvement is as much the global standard as the exception. Militaries as diverse as those in South Africa, Argentina, Pakistan, India, Mexico, and all the member states of NATO have contributed heavily when relief supplies needed to be delivered to remote locations, when survivors needed to be helicoptered to safety, or when the scale of destruction necessitated help from the central government in clearing debris and improvising shelter for evacuees. For example, the second biggest operational deployment of the Canadian forces since World War II was for disaster relief operations during ice storms in 1998. Other examples of military involvement in disaster relief include the post-tsunami operations of the Indian army in 2004 and the operations of the Pakistani forces after an earthquake in 2005. The Mexican army delivered relief supplies to thirteen Pacific Coast states after a 2003 earthquake and the Philippine army touts its commitment to response after the Mount Pinatubo volcano and various tropical storms.[1]

Indeed, in the United States as in most, if not all, countries the military is the arm of the central government that possesses the most manpower and equipment necessary to move large amounts of relief supplies into disaster zones and to bring self-contained and robust communications capabilities into places where the infrastructure has collapsed. The main difference between the United States and most other countries with respect to the military's role in disaster relief is that the U.S. armed forces have much more capability than other militaries. American armed forces have substantially greater transportation and communications capabilities than other militaries. The military's logistics system is also more robust than those in other countries. As a result the American military is better able to deploy quickly to a disaster zone, and coordinate and sustain operations in the field.

Examples of heavy military involvement in domestic disasters include the army's support for relief efforts in the Missouri River floods of 1881, the Charleston (South Carolina) earthquake of 1886, the Johnstown (Pennsylvania) flood of 1889, the Seattle fire of 1889, the drought in Oklahoma in 1890, and the tornadoes in St Louis in 1896, and more recently the floods during the 1990s in Washington, Oregon, California, Idaho, Nevada, North Dakota, and Nebraska.[2]

The most dramatic examples of military disaster relief in the nineteenth and early twentieth centuries are the army's efforts after the great Chicago fire of 1871 to help restore order and provide security for the reconstruction effort and, of course, the army's and navy's support to the response to the San Francisco earthquake of 1906.

According to some estimates, the San Francisco earthquake rendered almost 60 percent of the city's population homeless—225,000 out of a total municipal population at the time of 400,000.[3] During the initial response phase in San Francisco, army and navy personnel assisted in fire fighting and rescue operations. After the initial response, the army established and operated tent cities and field hospitals to shelter and care for earthquake victims. The army also took over control of municipal sanitation. Furthermore, medical and other supplies were shipped to the city from military depots across the country.

More recently, the military has been heavily engaged in the response to major disasters such as Hurricanes Katrina and Andrew and on both of these occasions the military level of effort dwarfed the efforts of all of the federal civilian government agencies combined. Indeed, Hurricanes Katrina and Andrew may have been the high watermarks in this regard. Approximately 17,000 army, air force, and marine personnel were on-the-ground in Louisiana, Alabama, and Mississippi within days after Hurricane Katrina. There were, in addition, another 11,000 sailors from the navy and Coast Guard who supported the relief effort. Naval ships, including the hospital ship, USNS Comfort with its thousand-plus beds, were deployed to the New Orleans and Pascagoula (Mississippi). Coast Guard conducted search and rescue operations throughout the disaster zone in small ships and helicopters. (The Coast Guard's rescue efforts were so heroic that historian Douglas Brinkley dedicated his book, *The Great Deluge*, to Coast Guard first responders.) There were, in addition, about 40,000 National

Guard troops from other states that participated in the relief effort.[4] The level of military support was almost as great after Hurricane Andrew in 1992. Approximately 23,000 troops and 7,000 National Guardsmen were involved in the Hurricane Andrew relief effort in South Florida.[5]

To put these numbers in perspective, the combined total of active duty and National Guard troops involved in Katrina and Andrew was 68,000 and 30,000 respectively. In comparison, 25,000 U.S. troops are stationed in Korea, still one of the world's hot spots, 7,000 troops are engaged in the peacekeeping operation in Kosovo and another 5,000 in Afghanistan. In other words, for a short time there were almost twice as many military personnel involved in Katrina relief than are in Korea, Kosovo, and Afghanistan combined.

Throughout the nineteenth century the federal government response to disasters was both ad hoc and essentially military. There was no institutionalized disaster relief program until World War I when the program was established as a military program by a War Department regulation. In 1917—during wartime—the War Department issued Special Regulation Number 67, Regulations Governing Flood Relief Work of the War Department which established the basic policies that would be applied, despite the title of the regulation, to all natural disasters. The War Department regulation guided federal disaster relief policy for forty years, until the disaster relief program was civilianized and melded with civil defense in the 1950s and 1960s. Importantly, many of the regulation's basic principles were retained when the program was civilianized and continue to be reflected in the contemporary disaster relief program. Before examining this regulation and its continuity with today's disaster relief policy, the relationship between the disaster relief program and national security deserves explanation.

During the cold war, national security was synonymous with deterrence and deterrence always had two aspects, active and passive. The active aspect was always the predominant one as the huge investments in nuclear arsenals, survivable command and control, and second-strike capabilities amply demonstrated. The passive side—civil defense—was always a relative stepchild in terms of funding, but it was never completely ignored.

One of the underlying and enduring assumptions of the civil defense program was that much of the investments in civil defense would improve the nation's capacity for responding to natural disasters. (This is, in effect, the reverse image of today when investments in disaster preparedness are presumed to improve the national capacity to respond to major terrorist attacks, the number one national security threat of the twenty-first century.) There was merit then to the argument because civil defense funding was used to provide federal grants to states for the construction of emergency operations centers and redundant communications capabilities that could be and, in fact, were used during hurricanes, earthquakes, and floods. Similarly, federal civil defense grants were issued to fund the development of nuclear evacuation plans that could also be used by a city when a hurricane was approaching. Although evacuation as a method of protecting big-city dwellers from a nuclear attack was widely derided as unrealistic due to traffic congestion and the widescale destruction that a nuclear exchange with the Soviet Union would cause, the identification of evacuation routes and the development of protocols for notifying the public did have value for disaster preparedness.

For a too brief interlude in the 1990s—after the cold war and before the war on terror—disaster relief was a stand-alone program in the sense that improvements in disaster relief were not thought of as secondary benefits from investments in more important national security programs. This changed in 2001 with the attacks on the World Trade Center and the Pentagon. The consequence was that the ability of the nation to reduce and manage the consequences of major terrorist events became as much or more important strategically as civil defense had ever been in the cold war. As was noted in Chapter 1, the capabilities that were developed for disaster relief as the cold war was winding down were adopted for consequence management even as new chemical and biological capabilities were being added.

Like nuclear deterrence during the cold war, homeland security consists of active and passive elements. The active components involve preventing terrorists from launching attacks against the United States by physically disrupting terrorist operations, eliminating safe havens and bases of operations for terrorists overseas, reducing the ability of terrorist organizations to raise funds, and by enlisting the cooperation of overseas law enforcement and intelligence agencies. Like civil defense in the cold war, consequence management has a lower priority than the active anti-terror measures, but because of the nature of the terrorist threat, a higher priority than civil defense ever did.

The nuclear threat implied complete destruction of both parties in the event of war between the Soviet Union and the United States, hence the concept of "mutual assured destruction." A consequence of the assumption that destruction would be "assured" was a certain level of fatalism about the utility of the civil defense program and considerable skepticism in Congress and among the public about the value of investments in civil defense per se. The terrorism threat implies no such fatalism about consequence management. Indeed, the United States has obviously experienced serious terrorist attacks and consequence management was demonstrated to have been extremely important to the survivors, their community, and the nation. The civil defense program never demonstrated such strategic salience.

In addition to consequence management—efforts to reduce or alleviate the effects of terrorist attacks—the passive aspect of homeland security also includes infrastructure protection. The focus of this book is on consequence management because that program is explicitly dependent upon the disaster relief system; but it should be noted that infrastructure protection consists of efforts to defend computer and communications networks, among other things, from cyber or physical attack, or to design "work-arounds" for key public or private sector capabilities that terrorists might be able to knock out. Infrastructure protection was also an issue during the cold war, but the sensitivity of the information associated with the program then and now is such that meaningful comparisons between the programs that existed in the 1970s and 1980s and the programs being implemented today are not possible. It is, however, conceivable that terrorists may be less interested in damaging critical infrastructure nodes than the Soviets were during the cold war because terrorism is by its very nature intended to create panic and fear among the public. Terrorists can achieve this goal by attacking uncritical targets such as schools, sports stadia, shopping malls, and commercial office buildings such as the World Trade Center.

Consequence management is defined by the federal government as consisting of "measures to protect public health and safety, restore essential government services, and provide emergency relief to governments, businesses, and individuals affected by the consequences of terrorism."[6] That this definition also describes the functions of the disaster relief program is no accident. The functions are basically the same and many (but not all) federal investments in consequence management will improve the nation's disaster relief system and vice versa.

The parallel to civil defense is again instructive. Some civil defense investments in the 1980s contributed nothing to disaster relief capabilities. A good example is the federal grants that funded the hardening of some state emergency operations centers so that they might survive a near hit in a nuclear attack. Obviously the extra concrete and steel that was required for the hardening made no difference to the emergency operations centers' ability to function during a hurricane or flood. The same cannot be said for some homeland security investments, even those that are designed for the terrorist threat. An example is the federal grants to fund the purchase of chemical and biological protective suits for the emergency medical services personnel and mobile laboratories for collecting or identifying potential chemical and biological agents. Protective suits and decontamination equipment may have no value in the response to ordinary natural disasters when there is no chemical or biological threat; but many disasters in industrial zones can involve toxic spills and the release of chemical gases for which these capabilities would be highly relevant. Investments in such things as communications interoperability and evacuation planning contributed to both disaster relief and civil defense in the 1980s and contribute now to disaster relief and consequence management.

There are, then, clear parallels between the cold war era and the era of the war on terrorism with respect to the relationship of the disaster relief program and national security. One particular place where a parallel does not exist is the political arena. During the cold war civil defense did not enjoy strong political support because opinion leaders and legislators regarded civil defense as either strategically superfluous or futile. Civil defense was thought of as superfluous by those who thought that the real work of deterrence was done by nuclear arsenals and that the Soviet Union would be (and was) deterred for reasons that had very little to do with the state of American civil defense capabilities. The program was viewed as futile by many civic leaders at the state and municipal level in the sense that nuclear war with the Soviet Union was assumed to inevitably be so devastating that investments in civil defense would make no meaningful difference in terms of the number of survivors.

Whether these judgments about the civil defense program were valid or not is irrelevant with respect to the question of whether similar judgments might apply to consequence management under homeland security. They do not, although in the wake of Hurricane Katrina there have been claims that the Bush administration has invested too much in counter-terrorism aspects of consequence management and too little in the disaster relief program, consequence management does not face the political hurdle that civil defense did. Unlike nuclear war scenarios, there is no doubt in anyone's mind that there is a real need for specialized equipment for chemical and biological threats. Indeed, chemical and biological weapons have already been used by terrorists. In 1995 the Aun Shinrikyo group used the nerve gas Sarin in an attack on the Tokyo subway system in which twelve people were killed and six thousand injured. In 2001 anthrax spores were sent to various government buildings in Washington, DC, and media offices in New York City by terrorists who are yet to be identified. Further in December 2005 four shopping centers in St. Petersburg, Russia, were subjected to a chemical gas attack that caused almost seventy people to be hospitalized. Media accounts attribute this attack to organized crime, rather than terrorists[7]—but the act itself plainly meets the definition of terrorism in that the targets were civilians (shoppers), innocent bystanders in the truest sense of the word.

In addition, the use of suicide bombers and, in the case of the September 11, 2001, attacks in the United States, airline hijackers who were willing to kill themselves demonstrates that a strategy of deterrence like the one that worked in the cold war and arguably made civil defense appear irrelevant has no relevance to the war on terrorism. Deterrence depends obviously and ultimately on the perceived threat of retaliation to the perpetrator. The strategy of deterrence presumes that potential attackers are rational thinkers who understand that massive retaliation was inevitable and thus would decide against taking steps that would provoke that retaliation. These conditions do not apply to many modern-day terrorists who plan on giving up their lives or hope to escape retaliation by obscuring their identity or basing their operations in countries whose governments may themselves oppose terrorism and thus cannot be retaliated against.

For all of these reasons, the connection between national security and consequence management will be more durable and less politically controversial than the connection between national security and civil defense (which depended less upon disaster relief) ever was. A likely consequence is that the military will become an even more important contributor to the disaster relief system. Indeed the military's role has already extended beyond the traditional one of supporting relief operations in disaster zones. The Defense Department also provides training to state and local government employees in the use of specialized equipment for chemical and biological incidents, maintains units that can be deployed on short notice to identify chemical and biological agents and assist in decontamination, and operates standby headquarters than can provide mobile communications support to relief operations.

THE 1917 WAR DEPARTMENT REGULATION

The most remarkable aspect of the 1917 Regulations Governing Flood Relief Work of the War Department is its consistency with the policies and priorities that are still embedded in the disaster relief program. Despite its title the regulation covered fires, earthquakes, and "other great catastrophe[s]."[8] The policies are outlined below:

Federal Coordinating Officials

The War Department regulation designated the senior military official in the military district affected by the disaster as the equivalent to today's on-scene federal coordinating officer. His (and in those days the senior officials would all have been male) responsibilities were to ensure that federal aid was delivered as efficiently as possible.

State Precedence

Like the current federal disaster relief legislation, the 1917 regulation recognized that state and local governments have the primary responsibility for responding to disasters and that federal (i.e., military) resources were to supplement, but not substitute for the state's efforts. In recent years, however, federal aid obviously has substituted for state funding. This is, after all, the necessary consequence whenever a disaster is declared by the president even though responding to the disaster was not "beyond the capabilities of the State and affected local governments" (the standard articulated in Section 401 of the Robert T. Stafford Disaster Relief and Emergency Assistance Act of 1988).

Federal Certification

Under the terms of the 1917 regulation, federal assistance would not be made available until the federal government determined that the disaster was severe enough to have overwhelmed the state and local authorities. In other words, the drafters of the regulations were reluctant to rely solely upon assertions by state and local officials that federal assistance was necessary because they recognized that the state and local officials would have a financial incentive to shift costs and responsibility to the federal government. Today's federal legislation also reflects recognition of these incentives for states and thus also requires a determination by federal authorities that disaster is actually of sufficient severity as to warrant federal action. As will be discussed further in later chapters, this particular requirement may no longer be cost-effective and should be reconsidered.

Under the 1917 regulations, the federal evaluation of the circumstances was to be made by the senior military officer in the district who would then forward his findings to the Secretary of War who would decide if federal assistance was warranted. This is analogous to the situation today wherein officials of the appropriate FEMA regional office conduct the evaluation and recommend approval or disapproval to the headquarters which in turn forwards a recommendation to the White House for a final decision by the president.

Cooperation with Local Authorities

The 1917 regulation emphasized the importance of cooperation with local authorities who were likely to be ad hoc relief committees of leading members of the community (elected officials, church elders, businessmen). Local governments are obviously more developed today than they were then and the typical disaster involves numerous municipal agencies: the Fire, Police, Transportation, Public Works, and School Departments to name a few. Municipal and county governments also have emergency management agencies (often actually only a single person) to promote cooperation horizontally among local agencies and vertically with the state government agencies and FEMA. Thus the networks for cooperation are, at least in theory, well established.

Accountability

The 1917 regulation established detailed accounting procedures that required the senior military officials to keep track of relief expenditures, personnel costs, and other administrative expenses. Today, the plans call for a "finance/administration section" in every disaster relief operation to track expenditures and prepare the accounting reports required by Washington.[9] There are, in addition, after-action audits by FEMA and the Government Accountability Office.

Avoidance of Waste and Abuse

The 1917 regulation required military officers to record the names and addresses of disaster relief recipients, in order to prevent duplicate payments. The current disaster relief program has exactly the same goal but fraud is still a problem as evidenced by the creation of a Hurricane Katrina Fraud Task Force consisting of the Department of Justice, the Federal Bureau of Investigation, the Postal Inspection Service, the Secret Service, the Federal Trade Commission, the Securities and Exchange Commission, and representatives of state and local law enforcement agencies. The task force was established on September 8, 2005,[10] and the first indictments for fraud were filed less than two weeks later.[11] In February 2006 the Government Accountability Office also criticized the federal government for financial controls of Hurricane Katrina relief payments that were "weak or nonexistent."[12]

Competition in Contracting

The 1917 regulation established a requirement that contracts for food delivery, debris clearance, etc. were to be awarded to the lowest bidder after proposals were invited from the private sector. There was also a requirement that emergency supplies were to be purchased locally in order to promote the recovery of the local economy. Under today's guidelines, the same general rules exist.

Equal Treatment of Minorities

The 1917 regulation specified that aid was to be distributed directly to disaster victims whenever possible. This was a response to reports of discrimination in past disasters in which aid was given to local relief committees who did not always distribute it equitably.[13] For example, after the 1886

Charleston (South Carolina) earthquake the municipal relief committee established a complex application process that had the effect of preventing illiterate farmers and homeowners from getting home-reconstruction aid. At the time, four-fifths of black South Carolinians over the age of twenty-one were illiterate—thus the application procedure kept most blacks from receiving aid.[14] Federal antidiscrimination policy is explicit in today's program, even though there have been criticisms of the way that minorities have been treated after Hurricanes Katrina, Andrew, and Hugo.

One aspect of military involvement in disaster relief that is not covered by the 1917 regulation is law enforcement.

THE MILITARY AND LAW ENFORCEMENT DURING DISASTERS

It is unfortunately, but perhaps understandably, the case that during the immediate aftermath of some disasters there has been a breakdown of law and order and state and local authorities have sometimes been unable to restore order without federal help. As is the case for disaster relief in general, the states have primary responsibility under the Constitution for maintaining law and order. Thus federal law enforcement assistance would ordinarily only be available after the state requests it. When the federal government provides law enforcement assistance to a state, it has often been in the form of military personnel.

For example, after the Chicago fire of 1871, there were widespread media reports of crime and violence. According to the Northwestern University and the Chicago Historical Society online exhibit, "The Great Chicago Fire," many journals at the time published drawings that depicted drunken looting and a 1892 memoir reported that

> in the midst of deserted saloons all kinds of liquors became free, and on Monday morning drunkenness and stealing added to the misery of the spectacle. Young men and old joined most recklessly in deeds of crime. In the south division, where great efforts were being made to save valuable goods, there rushed to and fro men mad with the prospect of stealing riches, and men mad with liquor, of all grades and colors.[15]

As a result, military support was requested and the army essentially took charge of the city for two weeks until order had been restored.

There were similar reports about crime and violence in the aftermath of the 1906 earthquake in San Francisco. In San Francisco, reports of looted shops, warehouses, and homes were so pervasive that the mayor issued the following order on April 18, the very same day that the earthquake occurred:

> The Federal Troops, the members of the regular Police and all Special Police Officers have been authorized by me to KILL any and all persons found engaged in Looting or in the Commission of Any Other Crime.[16]

In 1906 and today, federal troops can only be used for law enforcement purposes in certain circumstances. Under the Posse Comitatus Act of 1878 and its subsequent interpretation by the courts, military forces under federal command are not ordinarily used for the kind of law enforcement operations that took place in Chicago and San Francisco. The emphasis should be on the word "federal" as National Guard units are permitted to assist in law enforcement as long as they remain under the command of the state. Thus most of the time that military forces are used to enforce the law and restore order after a disaster, the units involved are from the state's National Guard and are under the command of the governor. Units from the National Guard of other states may also be seconded to the affected state and placed under the command of the governor of that state.

Since the National Guard can also be federalized—that is, activated under the command of the president such as the National Guard units that have been deployed in Bosnia and Iraq—the status of the affected National Guard units is critical in determining whether they can be used for law enforcement purposes. The "Federal Troops" that the mayor of San Francisco gave "shoot-to-kill" instructions to in 1906 were National Guard soldiers under state command and the U.S. Secretary of War issued instructions reminding their commander that "as long as you are assisting him [the Mayor], his orders must control, and you must conform to his judgment so far as police matters are concerned."[17]

The status of the Guard became an issue during the response to Hurricane Andrew in 1992. As reports of looting and outbreaks of violence were received, federal disaster response officials initially considered recommending that the Florida National Guard be federalized and then used to patrol the streets. Once it was understood that the Guard was authorized to perform arrests only while it was under the command of the Florida governor the recommendation was dropped.

With respect to law enforcement in the aftermath of disasters, the most important exceptions to the Posse Comitatus Act are the Insurrection Act and emergency authorities related to the threat of chemical, biological, and nuclear incidents. Under the Insurrection Act, federal military forces can be used to assist state and local authorities in civil disturbances at the request of a state provided certain conditions have been met. The Act further provides for the president to authorize a military role in law enforcement without a state request if and when it is determined that disorder is obstructing the execution of the laws of the United States and that local authorities are unable to protect the citizenry.[18] This exception has been utilized twice in the past fifteen years: once during Hurricane Hugo in 1989 to quell widespread looting in one of the U.S. Virgin Islands and again during the 1992 urban riots in Los Angeles.[19]

During the Los Angeles riots, the governor of California requested federal law enforcement assistance. As the Insurrection Act requires, the first step is for the president to issue a proclamation calling upon the rioters to disperse. If and when the rioters fail to disperse, a second statement—technically an executive order—is issued that directs military forces to assist in enforcing the law. Given the urgency of such situations, it is not surprising that the first order is largely a formality. The Los Angeles proclamation (Number 6427) and executive order (Number 12804) were issued on the same day, May 1, 1992. Even though Executive Order 12804 stated that "the conditions and domestic violence described [in the proclamation] continue and the person engaging in such acts of violence have not dispersed," it is clear that the rioters were not given much time to learn about, absorb, and act upon the proclamation before the troops were ordered in. The proclamation (Number 6027) and executive order (Number 12690) for the disturbance on St. Croix during Hurricane Hugo were also issued on the same day.

The other major exception to Posse Comitatus involves consequence management after nuclear, chemical, or biological incidents that occur as a result of terrorism or an accident, for example, at a military installation. The "Assistance in the case of crimes involving nuclear materials act" (Title 18 USC Section 831) permits Defense Department personnel to assist the Justice Department in enforcing prohibitions regarding nuclear materials, when the Attorney General and the Secretary of Defense jointly determine that an "emergency situation" exists that poses a serious threat to U.S. interests and is beyond the capability of civilian law enforcement agencies. The "Emergency situations involving chemical or biological weapons of mass destruction act" (Title 10 USC Section 382) states that when the Attorney General and the Secretary of Defense jointly determine that an "emergency situation" exists that poses a serious threat to U.S. interests and is beyond the capability of civilian law enforcement agencies, military personnel may assist the Justice Department in enforcing prohibitions regarding biological or chemical weapons of mass destruction.

HOW THE MILITARY ORGANIZES FOR DISASTER RELIEF AND CONSEQUENCE MANAGEMENT

Like many federal agencies the military is at once a centralized bureaucracy in Washington and an operational entity that functions in many different locations. Obviously the military's functions are performed both overseas and in bases scattered around the United States. The bases located inside the United States are, of course, where disasters directly affect the military. Disasters affect military bases in two ways—the bases can themselves be part of the disaster scene, or they can be the staging ground for military support for relief operations in other locations.

Many military bases are in fact located in and near ports that are in areas prone to hurricanes and tropical storms. Military bases in Florida, for example, are occasionally damaged by hurricanes. The naval air station in Pensacola, Florida, has for example suffered damage in back-to-back years from Hurricanes Ivan in 2004 and Dennis in 2005. Nearby Elgin Air Force Base was hit by Hurricane Georges in 1998 and Homestead Air Force Base in South Florida was destroyed by Hurricane Andrew in 1992. Recovery from the damage that disasters cause inside federal property such as military bases is the responsibility of the federal government and is of interest for our purposes only to the extent that destruction on military bases would limit the capacity of the military to support relief operations elsewhere.

Like any bureaucracy, in particular like any bureaucracy that functions in a political environment in which the senior civilian leadership changes every several years and the senior permanent staff (military officers) rotate from assignment to assignment every two or three years, the Defense Department undergoes periodic reorganizations. As a result of these reorganizations, the policy function for military support has shifted between the army (which has the plurality of the military assets that would be used in disaster relief operations), the civilian Office of the Secretary of Defense, and the Joint Staff (a unit of senior military personnel from all services who are assigned to the office of the Chairman of the Joint Chiefs of Staff). The name of the program for providing military support has also gone under several names—most recently "military support for civil authorities." The function is the same—determining how much military assets can be devoted to a disaster relief situation, ensuring that the request for military assistance is consistent with national policy, and clarifying the ground rules for reimbursing the military for the incremental costs it might incur—regardless of where it resides organizationally at any given point of time in the Defense Department.

Further, enthusiasm for the disaster relief mission has fluctuated over time for compelling reasons, principally concerns that overengagement in disaster relief would detract from military readiness by soaking up time that would otherwise be dedicated to combat training, or that there were not enough personnel to conduct disaster relief operations in combination with extensive operations overseas. This latter concern temporarily lost its purchase during the 1990s when the cold war ended and the military—notably the army—was looking for missions to justify its force structure and budget. The fact that the Clinton administration placed a higher priority on disaster relief than predecessor administrations was presumably also a contributing factor. The dawn of the war on terrorism and the concomitant national emphasis on consequence management have renewed the Defense Department's enthusiasm for disaster relief-related missions.

Despite these organizational changes and fluctuations in sentiment, the basic principles for authorizing military support for disaster relief have remained the same. At the policy level where the basic decision of whether to authorize military support or not is made, the first step is a request from another federal agency. For our purposes this ordinarily means the FEMA, but other agencies could request specialized military support in certain types of emergencies. For example, the Environmental Protection Agency or Coast Guard could request military help in responding to a land-based or offshore toxic spill, respectively. The policy decision about whether to provide the requested support would be made in the Pentagon after consultation with the Assistant Secretary of Defense for Homeland Defense about the legality and cost of the request and with the Joint Staff about the availability of forces. It is conceivable, for example, that during wartime the Pentagon might decide that it could not afford to shift troops to disaster relief work—although it is not very likely that troops would be withheld from a serious domestic emergency. Much more likely would be a decision to minimize the military involvement in an overseas disaster.

Once the decision has been made to authorize military support, a defense coordinating officer is appointed to work directly with the federal coordinating officer and a senior representative of the affected state. These three key officials are supposed to be colocated at a Joint Field Office in or near the scene of the disaster. At the Joint Field Office, the state coordinating officer would relay requests for federal assistance, including military support, to the federal coordinating officer who would consult with the defense coordinating officer about military options and—if military support was chosen—would ask the defense coordinating officer to convey the request to the appropriate officials in the military chain of command. Essentially the same structure would be utilized for consequence management after a major terrorist incident, only then there would be a principal federal officer presumably selected from the upper reaches of the Department of Homeland Security instead of a federal coordinating officer from FEMA.

The military command responsible for orchestrating the operational aspects of defense support to civil authorities in all its forms is Northern Command which was established in 2002.[20] Northern Command decides which units would actually assist in disaster support. For "routine" disasters, the ordinary course is for Northern Command to assign the relief mission to either the First Army or the Fifth Army. (The First Army and the Fifth Army are the only two subdivisions of the U.S. Army. As a result of post–cold war consolidation the Second Army, the Third Army, and the Fourth Army were stood down. The First Army and the Fifth Army have retained their traditional titles.) Headquartered in Georgia, the First Army is responsible for disaster relief operations east of the Mississippi River. Fifth Army is headquartered in Texas and would inherit disaster relief missions west of the Mississippi. Both the First Army and the Fifth Army have training support brigades which coordinate training for disaster relief missions and work closely with the relevant FEMA regional offices on an ongoing basis. Training support brigade commanders are usually designated as standby defense coordinating officers and are therefore, ordinarily, well prepared when disaster strikes and military support is requested.

For disasters that require a more substantial military effort, a Joint Task Force (JTF) may be established as they were during Hurricanes Katrina and Rita in 2005. A JTF is a temporary assemblage of military units from all of the services, not just the First Army or the Fifth Army, that are placed under the command of a single officer for the purposes of accomplishing a specific purpose—support for the recovery effort as in the case of JTF Katrina. In effect, a JTF structure is the military's solution to the problem of coordinating the activities of a large number of organizations, in this case different services and subordinate commands. When a JTF is established, the role of the defense coordinating officer changes into that of a liaison between the commander of the JTF and the federal coordinating officer and it is to the JTF commander that the defense coordinating officer would forward requests for military support that have been approved by the federal coordinating officer.

In addition the Defense Department is represented in all of the interagency working groups (emergency support functions) that may be activated pursuant to the National Response Plan described in Chapter 1. Given the many points at which the Defense Department and the military services may interact with disaster response operations, standing liaison officers have been posted at the headquarters and regional offices of the FEMA and at the Department of Homeland Security.

Northern Command has also established a permanent JTF (JTF-Civil Support) for response in consequence management situations that involve or potentially involve chemical, biological, or nuclear materials. There are also Civil Support Teams in the National Guard structure in the states that would, if federalized, be assigned to the JTF-Civil Support during an actual consequence management event.

Two other important aspects of military support to disaster and consequence management involve the Army Corps of Engineers and the National Guard which would ordinarily be a state, not federal asset in disaster relief. Although the Louisiana, Mississippi, and Alabama National Guard units remained under state control, much of the cost of their operations during Hurricane Katrina was assumed by the federal government pursuant to a federal law that allows for federal funding if approved by the Secretary of Defense and the reimbursement should, therefore, be considered as federal financial assistance to the state.

The Corps of Engineers operates outside the JTF structure, in part because its functions are so specialized, but also because it is the lead agency for one of the interagency working groups under the National Response Plan. Emergency Support Function 3, Public Works and Engineering, is led by the Corps of Engineers and in many disasters this has been a crucial function, as it was, for example, in New Orleans where the Corps led the effort to repair the levees that flooded the city after Hurricane Katrina.

The Coast Guard is also a military organization, but its enormous contributions to the relief effort in disasters should not properly be considered military support because the service is not part of the Defense Department. The Coast Guard is part of the civilian Department of Homeland Security and is, as noted earlier, one of the lead federal agencies for the response plan for oil spills and is thus one of the agencies that can request military support to civil authorities.

THE CENTRALITY OF MILITARY SUPPORT

As the numbers of military personnel assigned to Hurricane Katrina (almost 30,000 active duty soldiers and sailors, plus another 40,000 National Guardsmen under state command) clearly indicate, in terms of the amount of resources that it brings to the table, the military is *the* central federal player in responding to catastrophic disasters. The dollar and personnel value of the contributions of other federal agencies pales in comparison. Fortunately, most disasters require no military support at all and many of the disasters that do require military support require comparatively little and for very short periods of time.

Without the military, the federal government agencies would be able to do relatively little in the way of providing direct, tangible services to the victims of catastrophic disasters such as Hurricane Katrina. This has occasionally led to calls for the military to assume lead responsibility for managing the overall disaster relief system—but since the vast majority of disasters do not involve the military and, perhaps, since disaster relief is a program that is too often subject to criticism the Defense Department has been content to accede to the leadership of FEMA and other civilian agencies. Given the complexity of the response system and the intense criticism of the federal government after the hurricanes that are described in the following chapters, deferring to a civilian agency seems to have been a bureaucratically sagacious position.

Given the disproportionate size of the Defense Department's contribution to catastrophic disaster relief—the large number of personnel it can assign to a JTF, the vast amount of equipment and material it can bring to a disaster, and, frankly, its superior preparedness, and, judging from Hurricane Katrina, professionalism—the disaster relief system must appear as if it were designed to force a giant to be led by a dwarf. Indeed, the design of the system seems to violate an important principle of management— that primary responsibility for an operation be aligned with command and control over the assets most crucial to the operation's success or failure.

The FEMA nationally has about 2,500 full time employees and even if the entire agency were mobilized for disaster response, that would still be less than 9 percent of the personnel commitment made by the military in JTF-Katrina and only about 10 percent of the military personnel attached to JTF-Andrew.

Setting aside for a moment political and other practical considerations— such as the bureaucratic interests of the Defense Department, the concept of alignment in management literature would argue for reversing the relationship between the federal coordinating officer and the JTF commander during the operational phase of the response to a catastrophic disaster. If the principle is that the organization with the greatest investment should have the greatest say in terms of setting priorities and policies, then it might very well make sense for the military to assume the function of coordinating the federal response to a catastrophic disaster. This would, after all, be consistent with historical precedent before World War II. Further, the record seems clear that no agency of government does a better job of continuously preparing its employees for leadership and management under the stressful conditions of an emergency than the Defense Department. Indeed, a small, half step in this direction may have been taken after Hurricane Katrina when the civilian federal coordinating officer was removed and replaced by a Coast Guard Admiral in the fall of 2005. On April 26, 2006, the FEMA Director took what may perhaps be a second half step by designating five Coast Guard admirals as standby lead federal officials for the 2006 hurricane season.

Of course, the military has no role at all in most disasters, and other principles of sound management would argue against shifting back and forth between civilian and military leadership depending upon the perceived severity of the consequences of disasters and terrorist attacks.

Chapter 4

HURRICANE AGNES, THREE MILE ISLAND, AND THE ESTABLISHMENT OF FEMA

There were two major emergencies—one a catastrophic disaster, the other a near-disaster—in the 1970s that left a strong and continuing imprint on federal policy toward disasters and, indirectly, upon homeland security. The two were Hurricane Agnes in 1972 during the Nixon administration and the Three Mile Island nuclear incident of 1979 which occurred during the Carter administration.

These two "disasters" could hardly have been more different in terms of their scope. Hurricane Agnes directly impacted most of the east coast states, from Florida to New York, while Three Mile Island directly affected only one state. Ironically in both the center point was a single state, Pennsylvania and a single river, the Susquehanna. Hurricane Agnes caused more damage in Pennsylvania than has any other disaster before or since. Much of that damage was to communities along the Susquehanna. The Three Mile Island nuclear plant accident could have had, but did not, equally dire consequences. Located near the state capital, Harrisburg, and situated on an island in the middle of the Susquehanna River, the Three Mile Island accident had ripple effects across the entire nation.

In both incidents, the perception was that state and local governments were not as well prepared as they should have been and that the operations of the federal agencies had not been effectively coordinated. Dissatisfaction with the federal government's performance in both incidents, but particularly in Three Mile Island, led directly to major changes in the nation's approach to disaster preparedness and to new disaster relief policies at the federal level. Specifically, Federal disaster-related functions were reorganized to improve coordination and responsiveness; the federal government began to take a more proactive approach in working to upgrade the preparedness of state and local governments; and new regulatory policies toward the nuclear power industry were adopted to prevent the problems identified at Three Mile Island from happening again.

Before discussing these reforms, the incidents themselves will be briefly reviewed.

HURRICANE AGNES

Called by *Time* magazine at the time "the most ravaging storm in U.S. history"[1] Hurricane Agnes hit the east coast of the United States early in the hurricane season which runs from June through November each year. The storm made landfall in Florida on June 19, 1972, and worked its way northward to New York and Pennsylvania where on June 23 it merged with another weather system, stalled, and deluged the area with rain. Although it was only a Category 1 storm with wind speeds in the range of 74–95 miles per hour (not strong enough to cause structural damage to most buildings) when it arrived in Florida, the storm carried huge amounts of moisture. In fact, once it made landfall, the storm's winds quickly weakened further and on June 20, Hurricane Agnes was downgraded to tropical storm status.

It was as a tropical storm that Agnes dropped enough rain over parts of the country to spawn floods that exceeded "one-hundred-year flood" levels in some areas. In other words, the flood waters from Agnes were higher than the level of the worst flood that experts predicted might occur over a one hundred year span, or that actually did occur within the past one hundred.

Agnes deposited from six to nineteen inches of rain in the Central Atlantic and Northeast regions of the country. The floodwaters in Richmond, Virginia, were reported to have been higher than at any time in two hundred years—in fact the flood crested at six feet higher than the previous record which was set before the Declaration of Independence was signed. The previous record was set in 1771.[2] Harrisburg, Pennsylvania, was also flooded—the flow from the Susquehanna River was reportedly the highest that had ever been recorded in the city. Not only was the governor's mansion flooded and hospitals forced onto emergency power generators, railroad beds were washed out and sixty four miles of the Pennsylvania Turnpike had to be closed.[3] Floodwaters also invaded Pittsburgh, Scranton, and Wilkes-Barre, Pennsylvania, as well as a number of smaller towns along the banks of the rivers in central Pennsylvania and upstate New York.

One observer from the federal Office of Emergency Preparedness—the unit in the White House that at the time was responsible for coordinating federal disaster assistance—likened the flooding in the Wilkes-Barre area to the effect that would have been achieved if the Mississippi River had been forcibly rerouted through a tributary of the Susquehanna.[4] Cities along the river or one of its New York tributaries were also flooded, including Elmira and Corning. The city of Elmira was effectively split in two when it lost its main bridge to the floodwaters. As is always the case with major floods, there were widespread power outages and numerous washed-out roads and bridges.

The state of Florida escaped much of the rainfall from Agnes, but was declared a disaster due to the combined effects of Category 1 winds and rain. Six other states were declared disasters by the federal government due to the rains and subsequent flooding: Maryland, New York, Ohio, Pennsylvania, Virginia, and West Virginia.

Ohio and West Virginia were not declared disasters until more than three and two weeks after the storm, respectively. Thus the disaster relief provided to Ohio and West Virginia was reimbursement for state expenditures on flood cleanup and recovery and qualitatively different than the relief aid provided in New York, Pennsylvania, Maryland, and Virginia where food and water had to be distributed to tens of thousands of disaster victims and temporary shelter had to be arranged for the thousands of families who were driven from their homes by the flooding.

One of the reasons why Pennsylvania was the most heavily impacted state was was the fact that the state had had substantial rainfall in early June, thus the ground was already saturated when Agnes arrived and the additional moisture from the storm ran off into the rivers. Agnes caused at least $10 billion in damage (in 2005 dollars) and two-thirds of that damage occurred in Pennsylvania. Forty-eight Pennsylvanians died as a result of the storm and approximately 20,000 were made temporarily homeless by the floodwaters. Another 17,000 in New York and 10,000 in Maryland and Virginia were also driven from their homes. A number of cities (for example Scranton, Wilkes-Barre, and Elmira, New York) were evacuated based on flood warnings and many of the evacuees were among the thousands who lost their homes. Altogether one hundred people were killed by the storm and the number would undoubtedly have been higher if the cities along the Susquehanna and its tributaries had not been evacuated.

Much of the financial losses attributed to the storm were experienced by local, small business enterprises that were flooded out, but major employers were also affected. For example, the storm caused so much damage to its infrastructure that the Erie-Lackawanna railroad declared bankruptcy on June 26, 1972.[5] A less obvious economic impact was felt by the shellfishing industry in Chesapeake Bay where the Susquehanna River terminated. As the floodwaters worked their way down the Susquehanna, so much fresh water was pumped into the bay that the salt content of the upper bay waters was diluted to the point where oysters could not survive.[6] After the normal river flow resumed, the salinity of the upper bay gradually returned to normal levels.

The disaster effects were so serious that the governors of the most-affected states (Maryland, New York, and Pennsylvania) held a summit in Harrisburg on June 26, day three of the rainfall, to discuss the adequacy of federal assistance.[7] The summit was also attended by the governors of New Jersey and Delaware which had experienced significant, though less severe flooding. The timing of the summit must have had political ramifications as it occurred on the day after President Nixon had taken the traditional helicopter tour of the disaster areas. The fact that the governors were taking such a dramatic and public step led the president to take two measures. On June 26 he formally directed the Office of Emergency Preparedness and the other federal agencies to "provide all Federal assistance needed, and do it immediately by cutting through red tape"[8]—obviously implying that federal bureaucratic procedures were not sufficiently responsive to the needs of the storm victims—and on the 27th he announced that Vice President Agnew would go on a fact-finding tour of the states affected by the flooding.[9] The White House Press Secretary announced that one of the purposes of the vice president's trip was to "make sure Federal officials are cooperating fully."[10]

Curiously, the vice president was accompanied on his tour which started on June 28—five days after President Nixon had declared disasters in the most-affected states and six days after the rains had started to fall in the Middle Atlantic and Northeast region—by the same senior official from the Office of Emergency Preparedness who had represented the federal government at the governors' summit. Since the Office of Emergency Preparedness was responsible for ensuring that the federal agencies were cooperating fully in the relief effort since the president's June 23 disaster declarations, the decision to have him accompany the vice president may have been intended to give the Office of Emergency Preparedness higher visibilty and clout inside the federal bureaucracy. By virtue of the Office having been represented at the governors' summit and the agency's responsibility for assessing the situation from the federal level, the agency ought to have already had all of the important facts at its fingers.

In any event, during his tour the vice president heard what is now a familiar-sounding litany of criticism that the federal government was not doing enough to help the states meet the needs of the disaster victims or to begin the process of economic recovery. Among the facts that the vice president found were complaints that federal assistance to families that had lost their homes was inadequate. It was more than a week after the arrival of the storm and mobile homes were still being purchased for the homeless.[11] The housing situation was still so dire that ten days after the storm, on July 4, the Secretary of Housing and Urban Development issued an emergency appeal for housing for disaster victims and the press was still reporting that disaster victims still had to wait on line at Red Cross centers for temporary housing.[12] While these complaints were swirling, mobile homes that had been purchased were sitting empty and federal officials were being criticized for inconsistently applying the standards for reimbursing state expenditures. In effect, local government agencies were instructed that federal reimbursement would be available for certain expenses and several days later found that their claims for reimbursement were disallowed.[13]

Many victims of tropical storm Agnes remained in the government's mobile homes for years. Of the approximately 20,000 families in Pennsylvania who needed temporary housing, one-third were still in the mobile homes a year after the storm. By the storm's second anniversary 2,000 families were still living in mobile homes. This in turn led to criticism that the state, not the federal government, should have been responsible for providing the housing in the first place.[14]

One of the unusual features of the response to hurricane and tropical storm Agnes is the relatively subdued nature of the media coverage it received. As important as the storm's damage was, the press did not give it anywhere near the attention such a storm would get today (or that Hurricanes Katrina and Andrew have actually gotten). *Time* and *Newsweek*, for example, dedicated about as many lines of text to the storm as they do today to the review of a major movie. The nature of the coverage was also considerably more restrained than it is today. The fact that a vice president would not *start* a fact-finding tour until five days after the storm would today be sharply criticized by the media as callously insensitive to the predicament of disaster victims. Similarly, we know from press coverage of both Presidents Bush that today's media is highly critical of any president who even appears to take a hands-off approach toward managing relief operations after major hurricanes. As will be noted later, the first President Bush was criticized for not becoming more deeply involved in the relief effort after Hurricane Andrew and his son, the second President Bush, was heavily criticized for allowing the federal response after Hurricane Katrina to meander.

Another example of the difference in media coverage between today and 1972 is the way the press handled the speeches that the vice president made on his fact-finding tour of Pennsylvania and New York. While on the tour the vice president took time out to deliver partisan speeches on subjects that were unrelated to the disaster or to the relief effort. The press covered the speeches matter-of-factly, without doing what the press would do today—question whether the speeches were signs that the administration was not giving enough priority to the relief operation.

One reason for the different tone of media coverage, of course, is that the media today is simply more aggressive than it was in 1972. There are more media outlets today than there were in 1972 and competition among them has spurred reporters to dig deeper into the details of disasters—to look for human interest stories that presumably enable television viewers to connect with disaster victims and to expose shortcomings in the federal, state, and local response efforts. There were, of course, human interest stories in 1972 but there were not as many of them in the newspapers or on television as there are today. Further, in 1972 the press tended to pass along criticisms of the federal effort by state and local officials without amplifying them. Given the location of the storm—in the most heavily populated section of the country, near both the nation's capital and New York City, then by far the most important media center in the country—the media coverage of tropical storm Agnes seems all the more passive in comparison to the coverage of storms today.

A possible explanation for the difference between media coverage in 1972 and later disasters is that tropical storm Agnes occurred during an unusually turbulent period of time. During the summer of 1972 the Vietnam War and the antiwar protests were underway and both dominated the headlines during the weeks after tropical storm Agnes. Another major focus was the political conventions that were being held that summer to nominate candidates for the presidential election in November. The Democratic Party Convention came first and drew substantially more coverage than the storm. While it may appear surprising that in the policitally charged environment of party conventions President Nixon's handling of the Agnes relief effort did not receive more attention in the press, it should be remembered that tropical storm Agnes occurred before the era when relentless, round-the-clock media coverage ramped up the public's expectations of the federal government. Even so, political pressure on the White House to demonstrate results were nevertheless strong enough to cause the vice president to be sent on a mission to improve the federal response effort. Thus one of the lessons that can be drawn from tropical storm Agnes is that a heavy White House hand is sometimes necessary to achieve responsiveness and unity of effort within the family of federal agencies.

THREE MILE ISLAND

Labeled "the most serious" accident in the history of the commercial nuclear power industry in the United States by the Nuclear Regulatory Commission, the incident at Three Mile Island in southern Pennsylvania did not actually result in any deaths or serious injuries at the plant or in the adjacent communities.[15] It did, however, have serious and lasting effects on the industry as it changed the public's perceptions about nuclear power in ways that still influence federal and state policy today. In fact, the last nuclear power plant built in the United States was ordered before the accident at Three Mile Island. None have been ordered since. The public's anxiety over nuclear safety has prevented any new plants from being built, although this may change in the future as concerns grow over the price and availability of other fuels, especially oil.

In a fundamental way, Three Mile Island also caused the federal government to assume a more vigorous, proactive posture toward emergency planning in general and toward nuclear emergency planning in particular. In other words, like many of the major hurricanes that will be discussed in the following chapters, Three Mile Island resulted in substantial changes to federal disaster relief policies—even though it was not a disaster in the sense that tropical storm Agnes was, as it did not result in major destruction to private property and public infrastructure and did not drive thousands of people from thousands of damaged homes.

The Three Mile Island electricity-generation plant had two nuclear reactors—one of which experienced a partial core meltdown in March 1979. Whether the accident was the result of human error or was made virtually inevitable by the complexity of the safety system at the facility has been debated but is beyond the scope of this book.[16] It is, however, worth noting that there have been substantial improvements in both operator training and in the design of safety systems and procedures since the Three Mile Island incident took place.

Although the actual effects of the incident on the population in the surrounding communities turned out to have been slight—the incident generated high levels of public concern about the safety of nuclear power and the extensive effects that a future accident could have on the population. In fact, the incident raised so many disturbing questions about nuclear energy and preparedness for nuclear accidents that almost immediately after the crisis was resolved President Carter established a high level commission to examine the causes of the incident and to assess the government's emergency planning. The commissioners were given six months to complete their work and indeed the final report was issued six months later, in October 1979.

The commission's evaluation of the government's response to the emergency could hardly have been more damning:

> The response to the emergency was dominated by an atmosphere of almost total confusion. There was a lack of communication at all levels. Many key recommendations were made by individuals who were not in possession

of accurate information and those who managed the accident were slow to realize the significance and implications of the events that had taken place.[17]

The commission found that emergency plans of the federal and state governments were in virtual disarray. According to a paper written by the Pennsylvania Emergency Management Agency, the state Bureau of Radiation Protection was responsible for developing the emergency plan for the communities near Three Mile Island and other nuclear plants in the state. The Bureau submitted an emergency plan to the federal Nuclear Regulatory Commission in 1975 but the plan was disapproved and returned for revision. The plan had been revised, but not resubmitted to the Nuclear Regulatory Commission when the Three Mile Island accident occurred.[18] In other words, there was no approved plan, even though four years had passed since the state had been informed of the need for revisions in its draft plan.

Confusion about the actual conditions inside the plant led to a series of false steps on the evacuation of surrounding communities. For example, the governor of Pennsylvania was advised on March 30 by the state Bureau of Radiation Protection that the radiation levels outside the plant were so low that evacuation was not necessary, yet on that same day the chairman of the Nuclear Regulatory Commission recommended that the governor issue an evacuation advisory—essentially telling pregnant women and children to evacuate for health reasons. In the face of this conflicting advice, the governor erred on the side of caution and issued the advisory. There was also confusion about whether a second release would necessitate an evacuation of all of the population within a five, ten, or twenty mile radius of the plant.

At the federal level, the Nuclear Regulatory Commission was responsible for emergency planning for accidents at nuclear plants, but there was no overall federal plan. Moreover the Nuclear Regulatory Commission allowed nuclear plants to be licensed and operate even if there were no state emergency plan. As was noted earlier, Three Mile Island had been operating for years even though there was no approved state plan. According to the President's Commission on Three Mile Island, the emergency plans for the nearby towns and the county did not adequately address the issue of evacuation.[19] The evacuation plans for the three surrounding counties were only designed for evacuations of an area within a five-mile radius of the plant,[20] but during the event consideration was given to evacuations of much larger areas—areas up to ten and twenty miles of the plant.

The commission also found that neither the federal government, nor the operators of the nuclear plant had developed plans for providing information to the public about accidents—thus after the accident occurred "official sources of information were often confused or ignorant of the facts. News media coverage often reflected this confusion and ignorance." It was three days before the federal and state governments improvised a procedure to coordinate the information that was released to the public[21]—information that could have been critical if there had been a more serious release of radiation.

It is striking that the procedure that was improvised on day three of the incident to organize the flow of information at least inside the federal government bears considerable similarity to the process that is now used in disaster relief. An official from the Nuclear Regulatory Commission, Harold Denton, was designated as the president's "personal representative" on scene, akin to a federal coordinating officer or principal federal official. Special communications capabilities were also established to enable him to communicate directly with the White House.

There was, however, an important dissimilarity with the routine procedures for managing disaster relief at the federal level. At the same time that Harold Denton was acting as the President's on scene representative, a senior White House official was designated as the point man for ensuring unity of effort at the federal level and coordinating federal policies toward the state. The official was Jack H. Watson, a confidant of the president, Secretary to the Cabinet, and Assistant to the President for Intergovernmental Affairs. Watson and his deputy took the lead in coordinating federal policy toward evacuation and other response activities such as accelerating the acquisition of special, lead bricks that could be used to shield parts of the Three Mile Island facility from radiation. The authority for ordering an evacuation was the governor's, but a presidential recommendation to evacuate would obviously have weighed heavily in the governor's calculus—after interagency deliberation the president was not advised to step in. In an interagency meeting of the type that the head of the lead agency, the Nuclear Regulatory Commission, or even the Federal Disaster Assistance Administration might have been expected to chair, Watson reminded the heads of the federal agencies that their role was to help the state of Pennsylvania deal with the incident and instructed the Nuclear Regulatory Commission to develop guidelines for the state in the event an evacuation become necessary.[22]

Media coverage during Three Mile Island was different than during Hurricane Agnes because the two crises were so different. For one thing, hurricanes and floods happen often enough that their natures and impacts are generally well understood by reporters and their editors. There are, of course, technical aspects to the study of hurricanes—but their general features can be understood without mastery of a specialized field of knowledge and unique vocabulary. People understand that hurricanes are natural phenomena and are not anyone's fault. None of this was true for Three Mile Island. Three Mile Island was a man-made near-disaster. The details of the accident were simply not familiar and consequently were not well understood by the public or the media—and as the President's Commission noted, the government was not quick to help them understand. Further, the nature of the information about Three Mile Island was different in a nontechnical sense.

Coverage of hurricane and tropical storm Agnes was about facts: things that could be measured and that had already occurred. For example, the observed wind strength, the measured amount of rainfall, the actual height of floodwaters, and the physical damage that had resulted from the storm. Much of the coverage of Three Mile Island involved speculation about what might happen: whether more radiation would be released, whether explosions would occur, and what the short- and long-term health effects of different levels of exposure might be.

The *CBS Evening News* broadcast of March 30, 1979, by anchorperson Walter Cronkite included the following statements about what might result:

> The world has never known a day quite like today. It faced the considerable uncertainties and dangers of the worst nuclear power plant accident of the atomic age. And the horror tonight is that it could get much worse. It is not an atomic explosion that is feared; experts say that is impossible. But the spector [*sic*] was raised [of] perhaps the next most serious kind of nuclear catastrophe, a massive release of radioactivity . . . the potential is there for the ultimate risk of a meltdown at the Three Mile Island Atomic Power Plant.[23]

Even though there was no massive release of radioactivity, media coverage such as this had alerted the public to the possibility that there could have been one and, by implication, that radiation releases were possible at other nuclear plants. Thus media coverage of Three Mile Island had a substantively different impact than media coverage of Hurricane Agnes. Television broadcasts and newspaper articles about what might have happened in Pennsylvania in 1979 helped to create public demand for more effective government action to prevent such things from happening in the future. Although some critics, including the President's Commission accused portions of the print media of presenting an unnecessarily "frightening" impression of the accident (apparently through headlines and graphics, more than by the text of the accompanying articles),[24] other observes have concluded that the overall coverage was not sensationalist.[25] Either way, it is fair to say even if media coverage of Three Mile Island did not grossly exaggerate the danger, the mere discussion of the potential for radiation releases was enough to ensure that it had more of a political impact than media coverage of Hurricane Agnes.

The members of the President's Commission on Three Mile Island concluded their assessment by recommending to President Carter that the Nuclear Regulatory Commission be relieved of its responsibilities for developing a federal nuclear emergency plan and for ensuring that state and local governments have their own nuclear emergency plans. They recommended that these functions be transferred to FEMA—then a new agency that only recently had been established by President Carter after the Three Mile Island incident but before the Commission submitted its report.

ESTABLISHMENT OF FEMA

The FEMA was established in 1979 by the Carter administration in response to concerns that the federal government's disaster and emergency preparedness programs were too fragmented and had not functioned well after Three Mile Island and Hurricane Agnes. There were also more long-standing concerns about the effectiveness of the federal programs.

Because of these concerns, in 1977 the National Governors Association (NGA) set up a subcommittee to examine state and federal disaster programs. The NGA is what its name connotes—a bipartisan association of governors from all states that seeks to exert the governors' collective influence on national policy. Also in 1977, the NGA issued a policy statement calling for consolidation of federal disaster programs and launched a one-year study of federal and state disaster programs. In conducting the study *after* the policy statement was issued, the NGA was obviously not playing by the rules of the scientific method as the policy statement must have influenced the authors of the study as their collected and interpreted data.

Predictably, when the NGA report was issued in 1978 it included the conclusion that there were too many cooks in the kitchen where federal preparedness policy was concocted and that too many federal departments and agencies had a hand in disaster relief operations. The report recommended that all of the functions associated with disaster relief be centralized at the federal level. [26] Whether this conclusion and recommendation had been predetermined by the 1977 policy statement or not, the issues were real and the report had a strong influence on President Carter.[27]

The NGA report also reviewed the preparedness of the states and found, not surprisingly, that too many states were not as well prepared as they should have been. Since the governors were responsible for the preparedness of their states and the study authors were, in a sense, putting their bosses on report, the study couched its findings on the states rather diplomatically: "states should examine their capacity to deal with man-made and civil hazards in addition to natural disasters" and "many state emergency operations are fragmented."[28]

President Carter acted upon the NGA recommendation by consolidating the federal disaster and emergency management programs (emergency management is a term that was generally used to cover relief operations after things like the industrial accident at Three Mile Island) in a two-step process. The first step involved legislation to merge several small and specialized, emergency-related programs together into a new entity, FEMA. The programs affected by this legislation included two bureaucratic stepchildren from the Departments of Commerce and Housing and Urban Development that were only indirectly involved in disaster relief. The two were the Federal Insurance Administration transferred from Housing and Urban Development, and the National Fire Prevention and Control Administration from Commerce. Thus it is fair to say that the focus of the newborn, emergency management/disaster relief agency began to blur even before it was allowed to leave the test tube.

The second step was an executive order—executive orders are legal documents that presidents often use to delegate functions given by law to the president or to reassign delegated functions from one agency to another. One of the prominent features of Carter's executive order was the establishment of an emergency management council that was to be chaired by the FEMA director. This was an apparent adoption of an organizational model that had been in existence in a number of states—including Pennsylvania which seems a dubious model since that state had not been any better organized than the federal government during Three Mile Island. Many states, moreover, assigned the lieutenant governor as chairman of their emergency management councils. The parallel at the federal level would have been for the council to be chaired by the vice president rather than the FEMA director, particularly since FEMA was not an established agency and necessarily lacked the political and bureaucratic clout of the heads of the major departments (and, of course, the vice president).

This raises a point that will recur in subsequent chapters—the difference between what management journals sometimes refer to as "vesting" and "weighing." Vesting refers to the assignment of responsibility. The executive order vested or assigned FEMA with the responsibility of coordinating the federal government's pre-disaster preparedness programs as well as the actual relief operations during disasters. Weighing refers to the conferral of power—in this case the power to direct other organizations during the pre- and post-disaster time frames. The executive order conferred little such power to FEMA and sought to compensate for that in two ways. First, the executive order included the mandate that all of the federal agencies with disaster and emergency responsibilities were to cooperate with FEMA and with state and local governments in preparing for and responding to disasters. Second, the federal Emergency Management Council was chartered with the job of providing high level oversight of the federal government's emergency management/disaster relief programs and to provide advice and recommendations to the president for program improvements. This was an obvious effort to raise the priority of emergency preparedness government-wide, to institutionalize a mechanism for ensuring coordinated effort by federal agencies during disaster relief operations, and to enhance the bureaucratic clout of FEMA.

Despite these good intentions and perhaps because Carter was voted out of office a year later, the Emergency Management Council never functioned effectively and quickly became a vestigial organ in the body of the Washington bureaucracy.

In some very important respects, moreover, Executive Order 12148 represented less consolidation than meets the eye—even though it was endorsed by the National Governors Association. The Executive Order really only attempted to improve the efficiency and effectiveness of *preparedness* and did little to address the effectiveness of emergency and disaster relief *operations*. The executive order brought together three agencies whose responsibilities were largely in preparedness rather than operations:

> *The Federal Preparedness Agency in the General Services Administration.* As its name suggests, the Federal Preparedness Agency concentrated on working to improve emergency and disaster preparedness at the federal and state levels—largely by providing grants and policy guidance to states and by conducting exercises with states.

> *The Defense Civil Preparedness Agency in the Defense Department.* The Defense Civil Preparedness Agency administered the civil defense program—in effect nuclear attack preparedness. Like the Federal Preparedness Agency, the Defense Civil Preparedness Agency issued guidance and grants to states. The Defense Civil Preparedness program envisioned civil defense assets (e.g., emergency operations centers and robust communications equipment purchased by the states with federal grants) being used by state and local responders after natural disasters as well as in wartime.

> *The Federal Disaster Assistance Administration in the Department of Housing and Urban Development.* Like the other two agencies, the Federal Disaster Assistance Administration issued grants and policy guidance to states about how the grants were to be spent to improve disaster preparedness. As of 1973 the Federal Disaster Assistance Administration had become responsible for the operational functions that had formerly been discharged by the White House Office of Emergency Preparedness. Thus from 1973 to 1979, the Federal Disaster Assistance Administration

was in charge of coordinating disaster relief operations. Since the responsibility for coordinating disaster relief operations had traditionally been assigned to a single agency, the merger of the Federal Disaster Assistance Administration's *operational* functions into FEMA did not actually represent a streamlining or consolidation of the coordination function. A single agency was responsible for coordinating operations even before the Executive Order was issued.

Sections 2-201 and 2-202 of Executive Order 12148 established the ground rule that despite the consolidation of these three agencies into FEMA, many of the most important disaster relief functions would still be dispersed among the various federal departments and agencies.

> 2-201. In executing the functions under this Order, the Director shall develop policies which provide that all civil defense and civil emergency functions, resources, and systems of Executive agencies are:
>
> (a) founded on the use of existing organizations, resources, and systems to the maximum extent practicable. . . .
>
> 2-202. Assignments of civil emergency functions shall, whenever possible, be based on extensions (under emergency conditions) of the regular missions of the Executive agencies.

In other words, the executive order represented no more than partial consolidation. That may have been all that the traffic could bear politically and budgetarily. A reorganization in which all of the federal government's disaster-related operations were transferred to FEMA would unquestionably have sparked staunch bureaucratic resistance from agencies and congressional oversight committees. More importantly, such a reorganization would clearly have been both costly and inefficient. Partial consolidation was clearly a much more efficient approach than the alternative of building a new agency with operational capabilities that basically duplicated the capabilities that existing departments and agencies exercised during their normal course of business. For example, as long as the Defense Department maintained water purification equipment to support overseas military operations, it was more efficient to rely upon the Defense Department to help purify water during a disaster than to equip FEMA with a second set of water purification capabilities.

Partial consolidation is, moreover, an approach that the federal government has taken repeatedly in the past (and, continues to take as noted in the discussion of the National Response Plan in Chapter 1). A prominent example is the Office of National Drug Control Policy which coordinates the federal government's efforts to combat drug abuse and relies upon the operations of other agencies to achieve its goals. Roughly the same approach was also taken in 2001 and 2002 by the Bush administration in establishing a Homeland Security Advisor and staff whose responsibility was to coordinate the numerous law enforcement and intelligence agencies' efforts in the war on terrorism.

As the establishment of the Department of Homeland Security in 2003 has demonstrated, transferring operational functions from many agencies to a single agency is expensive and consuming. That may also have been a consideration when President Carter established FEMA. A more important consideration is that, despite the apparent frequency of disasters and disaster declarations by the president, delivering food and providing shelter and medical care to people disposed by a storm are not functions that the government performs on a daily basis. As has been pointed out, these are not even functions that are provided during most disasters, as most disasters involve nothing more operational than federal reimbursement of state and local government costs.

Thus while reliance on "existing federal organizations" made considerable sense, it left the new agency, FEMA, in roughly the same position as the Federal Disaster Assistance Administration had been with respect to its coordination responsibilities—particularly after the Emergency Management Council died on the vine.* The fact is that both before and after FEMA was established, disaster relief was a secondary or even tertiary responsibility of the "existing federal organizations" that were being relied upon to help states and communities alleviate the monetary and physical suffering of disaster victims. The Defense Department, the Department of Health, Education, and Welfare (now the Department of Health and Human Services), and the Department of Housing and Urban Development, to name three of the most important players in disaster relief, each were responsible to the president and Congress for a long list of functions, and disaster relief was not high on their priority lists. This is not to say that these agencies did not take disaster relief *operations* seriously, but rather that they did not prepare for disaster relief as sedulously as other functions during their normal course of business and ultimately had few meaningful incentives to work closely with FEMA until a disaster occurred. As every

---

* Early in the Reagan administration an Emergency Mobilization Preparedness Board was established to improve preparedness for wartime emergencies, including nuclear attack, as well as catastrophic disasters. The Board's primary concerns were national security preparedness. Disasters and industrial accidents like Three Mile Island were secondary or tertiary concerns. Thus, the Board should not be thought of as the successor to the Carter administration's Emergency Management Council. The author was a staff member assigned to the Board from 1983 to 1985.

disaster expert knows, successful coordination during a disaster requires cooperation ahead of time.

While it is true that FEMA may have contributed to this problem by uninspired leadership (as has been noted, the status and credibility of FEMA's political appointees have been subject to recurring criticism in the press and by Congress), the fact remains that the partial consolidation ordered by President Carter did nothing to change an underlying structural challenge that continues to this day. As we will see in the following chapters, many of problems that occurred in the response to tropical storm Agnes and Three Mile Island have recurred in the responses to Hurricanes Hugo, Andrew, and Katrina. After each of these "failures," the White House and the Congress appeared to recognize that the problems largely resulted from inadequate preparedness at the federal and state/local levels for out-of-the-ordinary disasters and from inadequate federal and state coordination of operations after the out-of-the-ordinary disasters occurred. Repeated efforts to fix these problems by fine-tuning the disaster relief system after each of these disasters have obviously not solved these particular problems.

As noted earlier, shortly after FEMA was created, it inherited emergency response functions from the Nuclear Regulatory Commission. These responsibilities were a good fit with the new agency's mission. FEMA was put in charge of developing a federal nuclear emergency plan which has since been incorporated into the National Response Plan—thus emergency operations after another nuclear power plant accident would be organized along the lines of the Incident Command System and a federal coordinating officer would be appointed to direct the offsite response—that is, the response in the communities near the affected nuclear plant. The technical response inside the facility would be the responsibility of the Nuclear Regulatory Commission or the Department of Energy or the Department of Defense if the accident were to occur on a federal nuclear facility. FEMA was also given the responsibility of ensuring that state and local governments had suitable evacuation and other emergency plans for nuclear plants and that these plans included the arrangements for the provision of accurate emergency information to the public. This responsibility closely paralleled the agency's responsibility for ensuring that the state had adequate natural disaster and civil defense plans during the cold war. Importantly, FEMA was empowered with what amounted to a veto over the licensing of nuclear power plants—the Nuclear Regulatory Commission was prohibited from issuing a license to a plant in a community that did not have approved evacuation and population protection plans. There is no equivalent power, nor could there be, over states with respect to the adequacy of there natural disaster plans.

THE LESSONS OF AGNES AND THREE MILE ISLAND

The governmental responses to tropical storm Agnes and Three Mile Island were less than fully successful as operations for a number of reasons—some of which were related to the degrees of difficulty that the two incidents presented. Three Mile Island presented unique, technical complexities simply by virtue of its being the first of its kind. The government was obviously not well prepared to handle this event. The underlying problem was that federal and state agencies paid insufficient attention to planning and preparing for emergencies of this type. To address this problem the Carter Executive Order directed that emergency and disaster plans at all levels of government were to be periodically tested and exercised to ensure that they were practical and that agencies maintained the operational capabilities envisioned by the plans. It made FEMA responsible for evaluating the extent to which the federal agencies and states maintained the requisite capabilities and conducted the required tests and exercises— but the agency only had effective power over the operators of nuclear power plants. Because it could prevent a plant from being licensed, the plant's owner had an economic incentive to meet FEMA's specifications for emergency plans.

Federal response operations in both Three Mile Island and tropical storm Agnes required intervention by the White House to achieve unity of effort among the federal agencies and to expedite support to the states— suggesting, of course, that at least in some major emergencies the federal departments and agencies do not heave together without external pressure from a source with greater political clout than the federal agency formally charged with coordination. This is a lesson that has been observed since— in Hurricanes Andrew and Katrina. It was also noted by the Commission established to review the the processing of intelligence about terrorist threats in the months before the September 11, 2001, attacks in New York City and Washington, DC.

President Carter recognized the disease but wrote a prescription in the form of Executive Order 12148 that did not cure it. The prescription was for centralized federal orchestration of preparedness planning at all levels of government by a new agency, FEMA. The executive order did not, however, give FEMA enough clout to overcome the low priority that is ordinarily assigned to preparedness. Nor did it address the issues of unity of command and coordination of relief operations, although the establishment of an Emergency Management Council chaired by the FEMA director might have been intended to provide a means for the FEMA director to obtain the political support that would be needed when the next Agnes or Three Mile Island rolled around.

In at least one respect, the policies adopted in 1979 seem fundamentally inconsistent with the lessons that had been observed in both tropical storm Agnes and Three Mile Island. In both cases it seemed clear that a small, low status agency (the Office of Emergency Preparedness and the Nuclear Regulatory Commission, respectively) had been unable to achieve unity of effort and that the vice president or another senior White House official had had to step in. Yet the Carter administration's solution was to leave a small, low status agency "in charge."

Chapter 5

HURRICANES HUGO AND ANDREW

[FEMA officials are] the sorriest bunch of bureaucratic jackasses I have ever known.

> Senator Ernest F. Hollings (D-South Carolina), Senate Floor, Washington, DC. Day 6 Hurricane Hugo response, 1989.[1]

Where hell is the cavalry on this one?... They keep saying we're going to get supplies. For God's sake, where are they?

> Kate Hale, Dade County (Florida) Emergency Management. Day 3 Hurricane Andrew response, 1992.[2]

These two quotes capture the frustration and disappointment that many in Washington and across the country felt toward the response to Hurricane Hugo in 1989 and Hurricane Andrew in 1992. This chapter examines these two events and discusses the reforms that were undertaken after the two hurricanes to improve the effectiveness of the disaster relief system. The quotes obviously imply that if certain federal officials, notably FEMA officials, had performed better the responses to both hurricanes would have been more effective. These views were widely held after both storms and led to political pressures for reforms that were implemented in 1993. In fact these quotes from 1989 and 1992 seem to have taken on lives of their own. The Hollings quote was cited repeatedly three years later in media coverage of Hurricane Andrew—it was, for example, used twice on one page in a 1992 *Newsweek* story on delays in federal assistance to South

Florida.[3] The Hollings and Hale quotes were also dusted off and used again in numerous press accounts of relief problems in Hurricane Katrina in 2005, as if they were proof that the problems that the disaster relief system experienced after catastrophic hurricanes can all be traced back to a handful of senior officials at FEMA.

There is no doubt that the federal government could have done a better job and that a more accomplished corps of executives at FEMA might have made a difference—but that difference would not have been enough. Disaster relief is a system of complex and interdependent programs that works well most of the time. When it succeeds, the disaster relief system does so not because of inspired operational leadership at the federal level, but because it is a system whose pieces have been built beforehand, over time in response to federal preparedness policies, state and local government initiative, and private sector response to market incentives and regulation, as well as the dedication of private voluntary organizations, and the acumen of individuals and families. Just as it would be a mistake to attribute the system's successes to the effectiveness of senior FEMA officials during the response effort, so too would it be shortsighted to assume that the system's failures resulted solely from actions or inactions of FEMA leaders in the immediate aftermath of a disaster.

One of the reasons for the relief problems that were experienced in Hurricanes Hugo and Andrew may have been that all of the human pieces of the system were a little out-of-practice, at least with respect to unusually large or powerful disasters. Three Mile Island in 1979 was followed by ten years of relative calm with respect to natural disasters, apart from the volcanic eruption at Mount St. Helens. While the volcano had a considerable economic impact (regional air traffic was interrupted and substantial expenses were incurred in cleaning volcano ash from city streets), its principal victims were the mountain's forests and the wildlife in the area. There was no need for a major relief operation to rescue, shelter, and feed large numbers of human victims because the area was lightly populated.

During the 1980–1988 period there were, on average, about twenty disaster declarations each year and most involved flooding and mild hurricanes. The storms that caused the most damage were Hurricanes Alicia (1983) and Gloria, Elena, and Juan (all in 1985). Each of these hurricanes caused between $1 billion and $1.5 billion in damage yet each paled in comparison to the damage from Hurricane Hugo in 1989 and Hurricane Andrew in 1992.

Hurricane Hugo was unique in one of the senses that Three Mile Island was. Just as Three Mile Island was the first of its kind, Hugo was the first of its kind for both FEMA and was something of a novelty for emergency management agencies in the states of North and South Carolina. It was, in fact, the first Category 4 or 5 storm to hit the United States since 1969, ten years before FEMA was created. It was also the first hurricane of that strength to hit the Carolinas in thirty years.

At the time, Hugo was called "the most powerful hurricane of the twentieth century" by the *UN Chronicle*—mostly due to its impact on the Eastern Caribbean where it hit first before crashing into South Carolina and North Carolina. Ironically, the United Nations praised the response of the Caribbean island states to the storm, noting particularly their cross-border cooperation and effective systems to alert residents to evacuate to shelter.[4] The feedback was not as positive in the U.S. Virgin Islands or on the mainland where conditions in the Carolinas made it clear that the reforms of 1979 had not succeeded in building a disaster response system that would be effective in a major hurricane.

Hurricane Hugo made landfall on the South Carolina coastline on September 22, 1989. Less than four weeks later, on October 17, there was a major earthquake in the San Francisco region.

Some of the after-action studies of the federal responses to the two 1989 disasters referred to the earthquake and hurricane as being "nearly simultaneous." This is, for example, how officials of the General Accounting Office (Congress' audit agency) accounted for the problems that were experienced in both disasters in a 1991 report to Congress.[5] It is a mistake, though, to conflate "nearly simultaneous" and simultaneous. The recovery efforts for the two disasters overlapped; but there were twenty-four days between the hurricane and earthquake and during the interim period the hurricane response was obviously not constrained by the yet-to-occur relief effort in California. Moreover, the most important and difficult part of a disaster response usually occurs during the first week or two after the event which in this case was well before the Loma Prieta earthquake struck San Francisco. Thus whatever strain there was from the near-simultaneity of the two disasters, it must have affected the response to the second disaster much more than the first. Yet the response to the Loma Prieta earthquake was not criticized as heavily as was the response to Hurricane Hugo at least in South Carolina.

The disparity between these two outcomes appears to confirm some of the points made earlier. First earthquakes are different than hurricanes and the public recognizes the differences. Thus the political expectations of the disaster relief system are different for earthquakes than for hurricanes.

Earthquakes occur without actionable warning; therefore government officials are not expected to take the kind of urgent preparatory steps that would be taken as hurricanes approach land. Government agencies track hurricanes every step of the way from their conception as tropical depressions off the coast of Africa, to their growth over warm Atlantic,

Caribbean, or Gulf of Mexico waters, and to their eventual dissipation over land. In effect, hurricanes telegraph their arrival to everyone with a television or radio, but earthquakes are always sudden and surprising to the people affected. Earthquakes also deliver their punch in a matter of seconds—too fast for anyone to do much other than to hide under a heavy desk or table until the tremors stop and too fast as well for government officials to even notify residents that they should not try to leave a building while the ground is shaking. By the time the residents could be notified, the initial tremors would have stopped. Hurricanes, on the other hand, can linger over a particular location for a day or more and the floods that sometimes follow later mean that a hurricane can continue to cause damage days after it has moved on or faded away.

A second point is that the relative success (or lack of criticism—which as long as there are no objective measures of operational success tends to serve as the single-most telling criterion) of the response to the Loma Prieta earthquake reflects an aspect of the complexity of the system. The response to the earthquake was a relative success because municipal fire departments had over the years developed exemplary fire suppression and prevention capabilities—fire, not the physical shaking of the ground, was the most damaging aspect of the 1906 San Francisco earthquake; utility companies in California were well prepared to shut off natural gas to damaged areas and expedite the safe restoration of gas and electric power afterwards; and the state of California had historically accorded a higher priority to emergency preparedness than most states. In fact, the General Accounting Office found in a post-earthquake report that "California's level of preparedness contributed to its ability to respond to the earthquake with relatively few problems."[6]

THE RELIEF EFFORT IN SOUTH CAROLINA

Hurricane Hugo was a Category 4 storm when it made landfall in South Carolina and its 135 mile per hour winds caused considerable damage in and around Charleston before moving west and north into North Carolina. Before it arrived in South Carolina the storm had caused major damage in the U.S. Virgin Islands and Puerto Rico. All told, the storm cost about $14 billion in damages (in 2002 dollars) according to the National Oceanographic and Atmospheric Administration.[7] Eleven billion of these costs were incurred in the Carolinas, with South Carolina being the more adversely affected state.

One of the important characteristics of this hurricane is its geographic span and the diversity of the communities it impacted. All told, 113 counties were included in the disaster declarations for the storm and most of them were rural, yet important cities (San Juan, Puerto Rico; Charleston, South Carolina; and Charlotte, North Carolina) also experienced severe damage. The storm wreaked havoc on heavily forested counties in South Carolina and tropical islands in the U.S. Virgin Island chain.

Despite the quote from Senator Hollings, it was not South Carolina where the response effort came up the shortest. That dubious distinction belongs to the Virgin Islands where the territorial government virtually collapsed and the federal government had to function as the first responder—not as the source of assistance to the local government. There was, in addition, widespread violence and looting on one island in particular, St. Croix, and 1,200 military police and U.S. marshalls had to be sent there to restore order. Nevertheless, it was in South Carolina where the shortcomings of the disaster relief effort had the greatest political consequences.

On Wednesday, September 29, a day and a half before the storm hit Charleston, the governor of South Carolina declared a state of emergency and recommended that coastal communities and low-lying neighborhoods be evacuated. The evacuation was generally successful although there were reports of traffic jams and overfilled shelters.[8] FEMA officials were deployed to North and South Carolina before the storm to facilitate the expected requests from the governors of both states that disaster declarations be made by the president. The FEMA representatives would also be there to coordinate the initial requests for federal assistance if and when the declarations were made. Curiously, officials in the city of Charleston may not have taken enough heed of these warnings themselves—the roof of city hall was cracked open by the hurricane's winds while the officials were meeting inside the building to discuss disaster relief plans.[9]

The disaster declaration process went smoothly—the president issued a declaration for South Carolina almost immediately after getting the governor's request. The declaration was issued less than twenty-four hours after the storm's arrival in the state. North Carolina's declaration was issued two days later. The state's request was also processed quickly by FEMA and the White House, but it was submitted later than South Carolina's. Once the declarations were issued, state requests for assistance began to be honored. The process, however, did not go smoothly particularly in South Carolina.

The exact reason why the process did not go smoothly is subject to dispute. Indeed, even during the relief effort there was some unhealthy finger-pointing by federal, state, and local officials. For example, FEMA was criticized by the state for not shipping enough generators to restore power while utility companies repaired their infrastructure; FEMA officials, in turn, claimed that the state had only requested a small number of generators and that those generators had been delivered on the same day they had been requested.[10] Perhaps inadvertently contributing to the perception that the federal bureaucracy was not sufficiently energized, President George H. W. Bush did not take the traditional presidential tour of the disaster scene until September 30, eight days after the storm hit— and one day after Senator Hollings had blasted the federal government on the Senate floor. From the perspective of the overall disaster relief system whether the state was too slow asking or the federal government too slow in giving is ultimately not as important as is the fact that the net results were unsatisfactory.

Four days after the storm only the hospital had power in Charleston and a third of the population of Florence (South Carolina) and half the population of Charlotte (North Carolina) were still without electricity.[11] Food and drinking water were also in short supply and hardly any of the storm debris had been cleared off the streets of Charleston.[12] A full week after the storm there were still 200,000 South Carolinians with no power and 50,000 residents of Charleston were still in temporary shelter.[13] Thus in terms of the standards for success that were introduced in Chapter 2, at least two were not met in South Carolina—substantial numbers of people were left without adequate shelter, food, or without water for more than 24 hours; and electricity was not restored on a timely basis.

A major complication in the relief effort in South Carolina was that communications at state and local level were disorganized, first because of the storm and second because of actions taken by the state government. First, the storm damaged many of the communications systems that state agencies relied upon to communicate with each other and coordinate their responses to the disaster. This not only reduced the effectiveness of the state agencies, because of the interdependency among the federal-state/local-private sector elements of the disaster relief system, it compromised the effectiveness of the federal efforts and may have had an adverse effect on the utility companies as they attempted to restore power. To the extent that poor communications slowed down the process of clearing downed trees and other debris from roadways important to emergency repair crews, the results were delays in the restoration of electrical service.

Second, the South Carolina emergency management agency was not as well funded or politically situated as its counterpart agency in California and thus not as capable. In fact, the organizational structure of the state government may have contributed to some of the problems that it expe-rienced. The head of the emergency management/disaster relief agency in South Carolina was not appointed by the governor but was instead an elected official. Perhaps because of this, there had traditionally been little oversight of the agency and its capabilities by the governor's of-fice. Further, few elected officials statewide had participated in emergency preparedness training or exercises. When Hurricane Hugo struck the state, the governor's office choose to rely upon the state police radio network to collect information about storm damage, rather than the network that had been set up by the emergency management agency.[14] Whether this was due to the governor's ignorance of the emergency management system or a conscious decision that the emergency management system was not satisfactory is unclear. The governor's office, of course, claimed after the fact that it relied upon the police network in order to reduce the burden on the emergency management agency.

Whatever the motive, the result was that there were two emergency operations centers in the state: one in the governor's office and the other at the emergency management agency, and there were reports that for ten days the emergency management agency did not even know that the second emergency operations center existed.[15] After-the-fact studies indicated that some local requests for aid were lost in the shuttle between these two systems.[16]

THE RELIEF EFFORT IN FLORIDA

Until 2005, Hurricane Andrew held the record as the singlemost costly disaster in the history of the United States. The third strongest storm to ever hit the United States, Andrew was a powerful Category 4 storm. As it cut across the Florida peninsula on August 24, 1992, the hurricane caused $35–40 billion in damage which was approximately two and a half times more damage than was caused by Hurricane Hugo. Sixty-one people died as a result of the storm.[17] Although Andrew went on to hit Louisiana, the bulk of the damage and almost all of the disaster relief problems occurred in Florida.

The number of homes in Florida that Hurricane Andrew damaged and the number of people it rendered temporarily homeless were unprecedented: 28,000 homes completely destroyed, 100,000 homes seriously damaged, 180,000–250,000 people left homeless. More than 80,000 local businesses were knocked out of commission due to storm damage and 1.5 million people lost electricity. Another 150,000 lost phone service.

The absence of phone service was an important issue, especially in 1992 when cells phones were not ubiquitous. One of FEMA's plans for expediting applications for disaster assistance involved teleservice. Telephone banks with toll free numbers were set up so that disaster victims could apply by phone. Obviously people who lost phone service could not call in to apply. Since many of these people refused to leave their damaged homes because they feared looting, were unable to travel, or did not know where to go, there were large number of victims who could not even apply for assistance until FEMA sent workers into the damaged neighborhoods to solicit applications door-to-door.

As was the case with Hurricane Hugo, a FEMA official had been deployed before the storm to Florida to facilitate the anticipated request for a disaster declaration by the governor and to coordinate the state's initial requests for federal aid after the president had approved the request. Given the fact that the request had to come from the state and both the governor and the main state emergency operating center were in the capital city, Tallahassee apparently seemed to have been the obvious location for the advance party of federal officials to deploy—even though Tallahassee was 400 miles by road from the disaster zone. On the other hand, 400 miles was too far away from the scene of the action. Indeed, if federal officials had stationed themselves 400 miles from Charleston, South Carolina, during Hurricane Hugo, they would have been somewhere between Richmond, Virginia, and Washington, DC. After a few days, a federal base of operations was established in a hangar at the Miami airport.

Again, as was true for Hugo, the declaration process went smoothly—the storm made landfall on the eastern coast of Florida during the early morning hours of Monday, August 24, and within eight hours the governor requested that a disaster be declared and President Bush issued the disaster declaration. According to the General Accounting Office, FEMA also assembled a small, interagency advance team and deployed it to Florida in a matter of hours—but then problems began to emerge. This was due, in large part, to the fact that the extent of the damage as summarized above was not understood by anyone or any organization in the disaster relief system. Local emergency management officials in the South Florida communities affected by the storm presumably had at least a partial picture of the damage in their immediate environs, but it would be a day or two before even they could quantify local needs and many had been unable to communicate even their partial assessments because their communications had been knocked out.

Despite the congressional and media criticisms that flew at FEMA like a flock of bats streaming out of a New Mexican cavern at nightfall, if any single organization was responsible for assessing the real-time situation in Florida it was the state government, not FEMA. Yet even after the heat of the crisis had passed, a General Accounting Office study faulted FEMA because the officials it deployed to Florida deferred to the state rather than leading an independent assessment of the situation and essentially dictating the results to the governor.[18] This criticism is unfair. By the terms of the 1979 Executive Order that established the agency, FEMA was "only" responsible for ensuring that somewhere in the system the capacity for assessing disaster situations, however dire, was being maintained (in this the agency obviously did fail) and the legislative foundation for disaster relief programs made it as clear as it could possibly be that the state had that responsibility. A state could not realistically have the primary responsibility for meeting the needs of its citizens without also having the primary responsibility for assessing what those needs are. Not only that, federal assumption of the responsibility for situation assessment after disasters would only invite states to do what the General Accounting Office and others have criticized them for—underinvesting in preparedness.

In any event, the needs of disaster victims in South Florida were not quickly met. Statistics compiled by the military and reported to Congress by the General Accounting Office indicate that

> Two days after the storm water and food were still in short supply; nearly one million people were still without electricity; and 35,000 people were being housed in inadequate shelters.

> Three days after the storm 500,000–600,000 were still without power; 20,000 were in inadequate shelters; and food and water were still in short supply.[19]

It was these conditions that drove Kate Hale, the Emergency Management Director for Dade County, to schedule a press conference on day 3 of the response to ask where the federal assistance was. It was these conditions and the storm of political criticism about the inadequacy of the relief effort that prompted President Bush to send a special representative to Florida to take charge of the response. That special representative was the Secretary of Transportation, Andrew Card. Card had a close relationship with the president, having served as deputy Chief of Staff in the White House and Assistant to the President earlier in the Bush administration.[20]

The appointment of Secretary Card warrants some discussion. First, it highlights the difference between vesting and weighing. A federal coordinating officer from FEMA had been in Florida for three days and was theoretically empowered as the president's on-scene representative to vigorously coordinate the actions of the other agencies; but the reality was that he was not perceived as being able to speak on behalf of the president and that a more senior representative of the president was needed to accelerate and coordinate the actions of the federal agencies. Indeed postmortem evaluations of the federal relief effort highlighted the fact that FEMA had not done a good job coordinating the efforts of the other federal agencies.[21] The Federal Response Plan described in Chapter 1, with its twenty-six departments and agencies and thirteen functional groups, existed on paper but was generally ignored in practice. As noted below, some agencies were simply unprepared for the missions assigned them and their burdens had to be carried by the Defense Department.

Second, it was another example of the need for the White House to take special steps to ensure unity of effort by the federal agencies. The other examples that have been noted so far are Vice President Agnew's fact-finding tour after tropical storm Agnes; Jack Watson's interagency strategizing in the Carter White House, and the appointment of Harold Denton as the president's "personal representative" during the Three Mile Island episode; President Clinton's flood relief summits during the Midwest floods; and the replacement of the FEMA Director by Coast Guard Admiral Thad Allen in the response to Hurricane Katrina. In effect, the White House has taken special steps after each catastrophic natural disaster in the past thirty-five years which suggests that a stronger White House role should be built into the process of responding to truly major disasters and not just repeatedly improvised on an ad hoc basis.

Almost 23,000 soldiers were sent to South Florida by the Defense Department to assist in the relief effort. As noted above, the number was so large because Secretary Card recommended and the president decided on Card's first day as the "tsar" of the relief effort that the military was to fill in for other federal agencies.[22] There were in addition almost 6,000 Florida National Guardsmen involved in the relief effort. Because the Guard stayed under state command it was not covered by the Posse Comitatus Act and was able to assist in law enforcement activities. Unfortunately there was enough looting and other crime that the police needed the Guard's help to patrol neighborhoods and maintain order.

It is hard to overestimate the importance of the military's contribution to the relief effort. They provided medical care to almost 68,000 civilians in the disaster zone and served 900,000 meals from mobile kitchens— in addition to distributing 1,000,000 prepackaged "meals ready to eat" or MREs. Soldiers built and operated four tent cities that housed on an average day 2,400 disaster victims and repaired storm damage at 98 schools. The military also removed 6.2 *million* cubic yards of debris from area roads, parking lots, and driveways.[23]

It is also hard to overestimate the importance of the utility companies' role although the story of the restoration of power is a classic example of a glass that appears either half full or half empty depending upon one's perspective. About 1,400,000 customers of Florida Power and Light in South Florida lost power after Hurricane Andrew blew through. While it is true that three days later 500,000–600,000 customers were still without power, about 900,000 had had their power restored.

Among the reasons why the local utility was able to get 900,000 customers back on line as quickly as they did were the company's emergency preparations and the system of cooperation among utility companies that facilitates the deployment of repair crews from the service area of other utilities into the disaster zone. Within eight hours of the storm's landfall, there were 800 repair crews from Florida Power and Light in the field and within twenty-seven hours after landfall, another 250 repair crews from utilities as far away as North Carolina and Pennsylvania. Another 650 workers from other utilities arrived within a day and a half. The arrangement for sharing emergency workers is something that is developed and maintained by the industry with no direct federal involvement. The industry's profit motive and desire to maintain customers' and the public utility commission's confidence in the reliability of the electric power system generate all the incentives that are necessary for repair crews to go into the field before the state or federal governments even think to ask about where the power is out.

In terms of the standards of success for disaster relief, most were not met after Hurricane Andrew. Despite the heavy lifting by the Defense Department and the utility industry, large numbers of people remained without adequate food, water, and shelter for days after the storm and hundreds of thousands were without power for extended periods of time. Approximately 200,000 were still without power after ten days. Finally, many victims experienced extensive delays in applying for disaster assistance because they would not leave their damaged homes and could not apply by telephone because their service had been knocked out by the storm.

LESSONS FROM HURRICANE ANDREW

I am outraged by the federal government's pathetically sluggish and ill-planned response to the devastating disaster wrought by Hurricane Andrew ... Time and again the federal government has failed to respond quickly and effectively to major disasters.

Congresswoman Barbara Mikulski (D-MD), Sub-Committee Chair, Appropriations Committee. House of Representatives, in a September 3, 1992 letter to the Comptroller General of the United States (head of the General Accounting Office).[24]

Apparently recalling disappointment with the response to Hurricane Hugo and perhaps Three Mile Island and tropical storm Agnes as well as Hurricane Andrew, Congresswoman Mikulski was not alone in believing that major reforms were necessary. Congress as a whole went so far as to require FEMA to contract for a thorough study of the disaster relief system with the National Academy of Public Administration (NAPA). Indeed the disaster relief system enjoyed a moment in the sun (for FEMA the sunlight was blistering) as studies about what went wrong in Florida and how to fix it became a temporary growth industry. As Congress, the Executive Branch, the media, and the academia shifted through the records to determine why things went so poorly during the first few days after Hurricane Andrew, the lessons that could have been drawn from Hurricane Hugo were more or less lost in the shuffle. They were, in any case, similar to the lessons that were ultimately drawn from the response to Hurricane Andrew and, for that matter, tropical storm Agnes and Three Mile Island.

Since Congresswoman Mikulski was the chair of the subcommittee that appropriated funding for FEMA, one might have thought that her views might have presaged a change of budgetary fortune for the now thirteen-year-old agency. That FEMA was not dismantled or shaken to its roots is one of the outcomes of the elections that took place two months after Mikulski's letter to the Comptroller General was written. The impact of the slow response to Hurricane Andrew on the November 1992 presidential election is beyond the scope of this book, but there is no doubt that dissatisfaction with the relief effort contributed to the victory of Bill Clinton, a Democrat, over the Republican incumbent George H. W. Bush. In effect, the elections gave FEMA something very much like a stay of execution as the incoming Clinton administration pledged to make the disaster relief system work better without, as shall be seen, making major reforms.

The most influential analyses of the response to Hurricane Andrew and its implications for federal disaster relief policy were the studies conducted by the NAPA and the General Accounting Office. The NAPA and GAO agreed that the principal problem in South Florida was that there had been no "timely and comprehensive system" for assessing damage and quantifying the needs of disaster victims.[25] NAPA concluded that the best way to ensure that timely and comprehensive situation assessments would be available in a future disaster was to establish a Disaster Crisis Monitoring Unit in the White House and joint assessment teams at FEMA.

The Disaster Crisis Monitoring Unit was envisioned as a small staff attached to the White House situation room with ready access to the president. Recognizing that a unit in the White House would be at least as dependent on reports from the disaster scene as the Florida state emergency operations center in Tallahassee had been during Hurricane Andrew, NAPA called for teams of federal-state-military officials to be deployed to the scenes of major disasters to determine the extent of the damage and relay a reliable estimate of the needs of disaster victims back to the governor of the state, the FEMA federal coordinating officer, and the disaster unit in the White House situation room. Although NAPA stated that the "essence of a team's operation must be speed;"[26] the report did not explain how quickly a few teams—even teams whose members were based outside of Washington, in the general region of the disaster—could assemble, deploy, and complete a comprehensive survey of a disaster scene covering several counties. There were references to using data from satellites and overflights by civilian or military aircraft—but joint assessment teams would not have to be deployed into the disaster zone in order to compile and interpret data from satellites and aircraft. These data could be analyzed in Washington as well as at ground zero.

While agreeing on the main points of the NAPA findings, GAO took a slightly different organizational tack, arguing that the functions that would be performed by the Disaster Crisis Monitoring Unit should instead be assigned to a new unit inside FEMA and that a senior White House official should be given "responsibility for catastrophic disaster preparedness and response."[27] Oddly, the GAO maintained that this official would not duplicate the responsibilities of the FEMA director although it is hard to see how it could have had any other effect if the White House designee had actually been assigned those responsibilities.

The other main emphasis of the NAPA report was that FEMA and the family of federal agencies should invest more resources and effort in preparedness. NAPA called for a long-term effort at developing the operations and communications capabilities envisioned for each of the many federal agencies in the Federal Response Plan. This recommendation was also echoed by the General Accounting Office. For FEMA this meant, among other things, run-of-the-mill recommendations for basic improvements in the recruitment, employee training, and internal communications. Recruitment at the senior levels in the agency was a particular concern. As the report noted, too many senior officials were political appointees and too many of them lacked the expertise and the stature that were necessary in disaster operations and also in coordinating preparedness activities. The NAPA report judged the political appointee "problem" to be so serious that it recommended that Congress pass legislation to sharply reduce the number of political appointee positions at the agency.[28]

Finally, NAPA clearly envisioned that the president would continue to send "tsars" to pick up the reins from federal coordinating officers during disasters. The report recommended that steps be taken ahead of time to improve the effectiveness of the Cabinet secretaries and White House staffers that would be designated for disaster duty. Examples of the NAPA recommendations were predeployment "orientation" and the provision of adequate "staff support" to the designated official on-scene.[29]

After taking office, the Clinton administration chose not to adopt the recommendations of NAPA and GAO. It chose instead to rely upon a new cadre of leaders at FEMA and direct presidential involvement in disaster relief as means to solve the problems of

> The inability of the system to quickly assess disaster situations when state and local assessment mechanisms are overwhelmed or otherwise fail;

Inadequate preparedness across the federal, state, and local government bureaucracies and an inadequate mechanism for evaluating their preparedness; and

Insufficient weighing of FEMA and federal coordinating officers during disaster relief operations.

Very shortly after the new FEMA leadership was installed, the agency was reorganized—itself a step that directly contributed nothing to solving any of the problems identified in major disasters—and adopted a more proactive approach toward disaster relief and disaster preparedness.

One of the shortcomings that the agency addressed was the finding made by GAO that the federal response to Hurricane Andrew was delayed somewhat by the fact that FEMA interpreted the Disaster Relief Act as allowing the expenditure of disaster relief funds only after the president had declared a disaster.[30] In other words, that FEMA could not authorize another agency to ship medical supplies or food to a staging ground near where a hurricane was expected to make landfall and would not itself ship supplies in advance of a storm. In the days before Andrew made landfall, the Defense Department had actually staged substantial amount of disaster relief supplies for shipment to South Florida, but FEMA would not authorize the shipment—and since Defense would not be reimbursed if it shipped without FEMA authorization, the materiel was not transported until after the storm.[31] As noted in both Hurricanes Hugo and Andrew, the agency did however deploy officials ahead of time to expedite the disaster declaration process.

After consultation with Congress, FEMA reinterpreted the Disaster Relief Act and began to incorporate pre-storm forward staging of relief supplies in the Federal Response Plan. The other major initiatives under the Clinton administration were a reduction in the agency's emphasis on cold war-related civil defense and an increase in emphasis on exercises as a tool for promoting and evaluating preparedness among the federal agencies and at the state and local levels.

As is often the case, when "new directions" are touted, the directions are not actually new. This was also the case for FEMA's "new directions"[32] circa 1993–1994. The agency's emphasis on exercises and preparedness evaluations had been recommended in the 1978 report by the National Governors' Association. Exercises and evaluations were also covered in President Carter's 1979 Executive Order. Both the NGA report *and* President Carter's press releases about the executive order also emphasized a proactive federal approach.

As important as these changes were, the decisive changes were in personnel not policy. The new FEMA director, James Lee Witt, had been the director of the Arkansas emergency management agency when President Clinton was governor and had expertise in the disaster relief field. Perhaps most significantly, he was perceived to have had a strong personal relationship with the president which gave him more "street credibility" than any of his predecessors or successors. This personnel change has been labeled "decisive" because for the first (and, so far, last) time the weighting and vesting of the FEMA director were roughly aligned. As a result, FEMA enjoyed something of a golden age—the agency was generally regarded as a turnaround success story—even though personal intervention by the president was required in the Midwest Floods of 1993.

One study actually referred to FEMA under Director Witt as a risen phoenix[33]—an odd metaphor, to be sure, as it implies a return to the status quo ante. With respect to catastrophic disasters, there was no acceptable status quo ante.

For the reasons noted in Chapter 1, the fact that FEMA and the disaster relief system functioned reasonably well during the 1990s does not, however, mean that it would have been able to handle a storm as powerful as Hurricane Andrew or Hurricane Katrina. Indeed, although the agency under Director Witt deserves credit for acquitting itself well in the Loma Prieta and North Ridge earthquakes and, with the personal intervention of the president, the Midwest floods; it did not face any hurricane as powerful as Andrew or Katrina during the Clinton presidency.

The disaster relief system still had so many moving pieces at each of the three levels of government (federal, state, local) and in the private sector that orchestrating their operations during disasters and cajoling them into continual investment in preparedness were still challenges that were not being fully met during the Clinton administration and received even lower priority after he left office. Further the problem of quickly obtaining a comprehensive situation assessment when the state and local governments are unable to evaluate the extent of damage and the needs of disaster victims was not solved during the 1990s. Judging from the confusion attending the response to Hurricane Katrina in 2005, the problem has not been solved since. Further, nothing that was done during the period between Hurricanes Andrew and Katrina altered the disaster relief system's heavy dependence upon the ability of the private sector to restore power and other utilities, quickly pay insurance claims, and provide temporary food and shelter to disaster victims.

Chapter 6

HURRICANE KATRINA

The preparation and response to Hurricane Katrina show we are still in an analog government in a digital age.
> Select Bipartisan Committee to Investigate the Preparations for and Response to Hurricane Katrina, U.S. House of Representatives, February 15, 2006.

Help us, Please.
> The headline of The Times-Picayune, New Orleans, September 2, 2005. Four days after Katrina's landfall.

Unfortunately, many of the lessons emerging from the most recent hurricanes in the Gulf are similar to those GAO identified more than a decade ago, in the aftermath of Hurricane Andrew, which leveled much of South Florida in the early 1990s.
> David M. Walker, Comptroller General of the United States, Letter to Congress, February 1, 2006.

In terms of the damage it caused and its long-term consequences, there truly has been nothing to compare to Hurricane Katrina. There has also been nothing that compares to the extent of the failure of the disaster relief system in responding to this hurricane. The system was initially overwhelmed— not unlike the situations in Hurricanes Hugo and Andrew—and unfortunately took longer to catch up with the needs of disaster victims than had been the case in any of the other disasters touched upon in this book.

Indeed, six months after the storm hit New Orleans large numbers of disaster victims had not only been unable to return to their homes, their temporary housing was still being paid for by federal disaster relief funds. By the sixth month after the storm, FEMA had spent a total of $529 million in hotel and motel rooms for disaster victims and 8,900 hotel or motel rooms in Louisiana were still being occupied by disaster victims whose rent was being paid by FEMA. There were also still 40,000 people residing in FEMA trailers in Louisiana.[1]

The extent of the storm's damage and its effects upon the people living in the three states and more than 90,000 square miles the storm affected were principally due, of course, to the strength of the storm and the unique features of the terrain where it made landfall. It is well known that the low-lying city of New Orleans is in a geographically precarious location, surrounded as it is by water and dependent for its survival on a series of levees and pumps that keep the city dry.

Another factor was that there were rising expectations of the government, in particular of the federal government which had launched an aggressive reorganization after the September 11, 2001 terrorist attacks to improve its response to all types of domestic emergencies and which had theoretically learned from the preparedness exercises that had been conducted during the Clinton administration and which, indeed, continued after the Bush administration took office. Further, since the hurricane hit a part of the country that has as much experience with storms as any other region, there should have been a high level of awareness among the public and within the local governments about how to prepare for a hurricane and what to do after it arrived. In fact, only a year before Hurricane Katrina there had actually been a preparedness exercise in Louisiana for a storm that bore a remarkable resemblance to Hurricane Katrina. The faux-storm was roughly the same strength as Katrina turned out to be, and the exercise scenario even envisioned the kind of flooding in New Orleans that turned out to be the biggest obstacle in the response to Katrina. There was, in addition, another major exercise in New Orleans during the 1990s and the scenario for that exercise also envisioned that the city would be flooded. Aside from these exercises, the dangerous conditions of the levees in New Orleans and their susceptibility to storm damage were hardly news in 2006. For years before Hurricane Katrina there had been numerous studies of the disastrous effects that levee failure would have on the city.

Of course, none of these factors mattered very much when Katrina attacked the Gulf Coast and the fact that governments at all levels proved to be ill-prepared has understandably raised concern about the design of the disaster relief system, as is evidenced by the quote at the beginning of this chapter about our having an analog system in a digital age. This quote was specifically about the system's ability to obtain and process large amounts of data during a crisis, but it has deep implications for the basic design of the system because the design of the system itself creates data complexity. However, it must be noted that much of the problem in the very early stages of the response to Katrina was not too much complex information, but too little—specifically, too little information about the extent of the storm damage and the immediate needs of disaster victims. These are, of course, exactly the same things that were unclear in the immediate aftermath of Hurricanes Andrew and Hugo.

THE STORM

Hurricane Katrina first hit Florida on August 25, 2005, and then moved out into the Gulf of Mexico where it spent a few days building strength over the warm water. After it had built itself up to Category 5 strength the storm moved toward the Gulf Coast, but fortunately weakened to borderline Category 4 or Category 3 just before it made landfall on Monday, August 29. Incredibly the storm had a diameter of more than 200 miles, so when it hit the Gulf Coast a large geographic area was immediately affected.

The approach of the storm was well advertised and Louisiana, Mississippi, and Alabama each took important preparatory actions in the days before landfall. Each of the states suggested voluntary evacuations, opened emergency shelters, prepositioned emergency supplies in the shelters, alerted National Guard forces, and activated emergency operations centers. An impressive total of 1.2 million people evacuated New Orleans and its environs. The evacuations went so smoothly (especially in comparison to much smaller evacuations in South Carolina during the approach of Hurricanes Bertha and Fran in 1996 in which there were highly publicized traffic jams) that on the day before landfall, "contraflow" on major roads was lifted.[2] Contraflow is the term of art for temporarily converting inbound lanes on major roads to outbound traffic (or vice versa) to facilitate evacuations.

FEMA, the military, and various nongovernmental organizations also took significant preparatory steps before the storm hit. Thirty-one medical response teams were alerted and prepositioned in neighboring states so that they could be on scene almost immediately after the storm passed. Over 11 million liters of water, 9 million pounds of ice, and 5.9 million "meals ready to eat" were also prepositioned so that they could be made available quickly to disaster victims.[3] That these preparations turned out to have been inadequate does not mean that they should be dismissed as inconsequential—in fact they represented a considerable effort on the part of the various elements of the disaster response system.

As effective as the evacuation of New Orleans was, it obviously only helped those who moved to safer locations and it turned out that many thousands of New Orleans residents either were unable to leave the city or chose not to because they doubted the predictions about the storm's intensity. Their doubts might have been at least partially based upon the fact that the mayor did not order a mandatory evacuation until the day before the storm hit, ultimately leaving it up to the people who had not already left to decide whether to even try to leave the city. The city did not have a full evacuation plan and the arrangements it made to transport the tens of thousands who had not already evacuated and who did not have cars were clearly inadequate. When the mayor announced the mandatory evacuation, he declared that school buses would ferry residents from 12 different pick-up sites to a shelter. However, the sites were not marked and the buses stopped running after only a couple of hours—leaving many thousands of residents in the lurch.[4] Thus, despite all of the state precautions and the federal prepositioning of emergency teams and supplies, the system was woefully ill-equipped to take care of the people who stayed behind. Once the levees broke, which happened soon after the storm hit, thousands of people were isolated in city neighborhoods. The rising water in the streets forced stranded families to move to the second floors and roofs of homes where they had to wait for rescue by personnel from city, state, and federal government agencies (most notably, the Coast Guard which had deployed 4,000 guardsmen, 37 aircraft, and 78 boats of various size to the area[5]) who had not even known which buildings were still occuppied and, moreover, had limited transportation capabilities due to the high waters and storm damage. The flood waters also stranded thousands of physicians, staff, and patients in power-less hospitals and medical centers throughout the city.[6] It was several days before all of them could be evacuated.

New Orleans' emergency plans designated the city's enclosed sports stadium, the Superdome, as one of the main shelters, and as the storm approached it was designated as the primary shelter for people who had not been able to evacuate. However, the city did not anticipate the large number of people who would eventually come to the Superdome, nor did it envision that the people would stay in the stadium for as long as they did. The emergency plans envisioned sheltering several thousand people for a short period of time—until the storm passed and they could return to their homes, or until they could be evacuated to a more suitable shelter.

Ultimately, approximately 30,000 people ended up in the Superdome, most arriving the day before the storm, others being ferried there in the following days after being rescued by boat from flooded neighborhoods. Most of the 30,000 were stuck there for three days in the sweltering heat without sanitary facilities or enough food and water. Another 20,000 were at the New Orleans Convention Center under better, but still unsatisfactory conditions.

Media coverage of the situation in the Superdome highlighted the abominable conditions that the "refugees" had to endure. As the Cable News Network reported

> Rumors of violence and chaos at the Superdome abound—one man is reported to have calmly leaped from the second-level bleachers to his death—but reports vary and some say the atmosphere is "not too horrific." Toilets have been overflowing for two days. The heat is intolerable. Many are ill and in need of medical attention. There is no drinking water.[7]

Indeed, media coverage and even statements by city officials including the mayor and the police chief suggested that anarchy reigned inside the Superdome and that the evacuees were being terrorized by the violent criminals inside the stadium. While it turned out that the reports of violence inside the Superdome were exaggerated, as the media and the city officials conceded in late September 2005,[8] there is no doubt that the Superdome and the Convention Center were dangerous places for families. The National Guardsmen who eventually went in to police the sites reported that many of the people in the buildings had been filling their time by drinking alcohol that had been looted from nearby stores.[9] The Superdome reports and the verified reports of looting and violence in other parts of the city were enough to confirm to the general public the sense that the disaster relief system had fallen apart. Indeed the municipal police department had literally fallen apart. On the one hand, the department's capability was reduced by equipment lost to the storm and personnel who either could not get to work or simply failed to report and, on the other, its missions were expanded beyond the point that even the pre-hurricane police force could have handled. The downsized department could not both patrol the streets in enough number to suppress looting and at the same time search neighborhoods for people who were still stranded. It was not until the fourth and fifth day after the storm that the National Guard and the police were able to restore order.

After the third day when the water levels on the key city streets were starting to fall, evacuation from the Convention Center and Superdome to shelters as far away as New England began although stragglers continued to make their way to the stadium as late as September 4, a week after the storm's landfall. Altogether more than 200,000 disaster victims were resettled at least temporarily in Texas, another 50,000 in Arkansas and 12,000 in Tennessee.

Rescuing city residents from flooded houses and getting the occupants of the Superdome and Convention Center into adequate shelters were not the only major problems posed by Hurricane Katrina. The storm caused extensive damage to private houses, businesses—including oil platforms off the coast of Louisiana that were torn loose from their moorings—and public infrastructure. The storm also created tremendous personal hardship for hundreds of thousands of disaster victims and caused at least 1,300 deaths. Between 1.4 and 1.7 million households received financial assistance directly from the FEMA[10] as well as assistance from other federal agencies and nongovernment sources. Approximately 400,000 people were driven from their homes by the storm or the subsequent flooding. A February 2006 report issued by the White House estimated 300,000 homes had been destroyed or made "uninhabitable" by the storm.[11]

One way to characterize the relief effort in the Gulf States, in particular, in and around New Orleans, would be to catalogue the statistics about such things as the total dollar value of the various forms of vouchers and debit cards that were distributed to disaster victims, or the number of meals that were served to victims and relief workers, and the number of victims that were housed in shelters. Some of these data will be merely provided to convey a sense of the Herculean level of effort that was expended, but as impressive as the effort was, it was not nearly enough. As will be discussed below, it is also clear that the relief effort did not accelerate as quickly as it could have and should have.

As was observed in Chapter 3, the military played a major role in the response effort. According to the Assistant Secretary of Defense for Homeland Defense, Hurricane Katrina relief was the largest military operation inside the United States since the Civil War.[12] The high watermark for military forces in the relief effort was about 70,000 of which about 40,000 were National Guardsmen operating under state, not federal command.

The majority of National Guardsmen in the Katrina relief effort were from states other than three affected states—testimony to the effectiveness of the Emergency Management Assistance Compact arrangements that states have negotiated for sharing assets. The table below applies to Louisiana, but the trend of the gradual ramping up of support from other states applies to Mississippi as well. Alabama was less impacted by the storm and thus was one of the states that provided military support to Mississippi and Louisiana.

National Guard Deployments in Louisiana

	Louisiana Guard	Other States
August 30	5,804	178
August 31	5,804	663
September 1	5,804	2,555
September 2	6,779	5,445
September 3	6,779	10,635
September 4	6,779	12,404
September 5	6,779	16,162
September 6	6,779	20,510
September 7	6,779	22,589
September 8	6,779	23,476[13]

National Guard personnel from as far away as Puerto Rico, Massachusetts, and Oregon were involved in the relief operations.

An interesting sidelight of the military's role was that FEMA actually asked the military to take over one of the functions it had assigned to itself in the National Response Plan, recalling the military's assumption of other civilian agencies' responsibilities after Hurricane Andrew. This particular function was managing the distribution of relief supplies from depots in and near the disaster zone—obviously one of the very basic functions upon which much else depends.[14] FEMA's inability to discharge this function may be another sign that the emergency plans are simply too complex for out-of-the-ordinary disasters. It may also be a sign that no one agency may be able to perform all of the disaster relief functions that have been assigned to FEMA or that the agency has assigned to itself:

Coordinate the activities of a large number of other federal agencies—each with subagencies and multiple programs;

Work hand in glove with the affected states which are themselves under duress and struggling to manage their own sets of agencies and local governments;

Administer its own programs for providing assistance directly to large numbers of disaster victims, all the while under great pressure to accommodate victims as quickly as humanly possible;

Manage the distribution of relief supplies; and

Influence/orchestrate the efforts of nongovernmental organizations and private sector relief efforts.

With respect to the nongovernmental organizations, it should be noted that their contributions were substantial. The Red Cross opened 239 shelters to house almost 40,000 of the evacuees on the same day that the storm made landfall and opened almost 300 more shelters over the following week. By September 8 the number of Red Cross shelters peaked at 527 and the number of sheltered evacuees at more than 140,000. The rate of increase in sheltering during the first few days after the hurricane is depicted in the following table.

Red Cross Shelters

Date	Shelters	Population
August 29	239	37,091
August 30	254	41,013
August 31	259	52,719
September 1	275	76,453
September 2	308	94,308
September 3	361	96,178
September 4	397	106,970
September 5	413	124,617
September 6	490	125,941
September 7	504	143,712
September 8	527	138,294[15]

The Salvation Army sheltered another 30,000 disaster victims in its 225 shelters.[16] The Red Cross also distributed or served through mobile kitchens (which were staffed by volunteers from the Southern Baptists organization) 31 million meals and its last mobile kitchen continued to serve meals until February 15, 2006—almost six months after the storm.[17] The Salvation Army operated 178 canteens and 11 mobile kitchens that served 20,000 meals per day. The Red Cross and the Salvation Army paid for the cost of these operations through donations from private citizens and corporations. The total amount of donated funds that the Red Cross expended on shelter, feeding, and other forms of relief was approximately $3 billion.[18]

To put the statistics on sheltering and feeding in perspective, three points must be made. The first is that arranging shelter for up to 170,000 evacuees on short notice would be a major accomplishment for any organization, in particular a nongovernment organization. Secondly, it was a major contribution to the disaster response. Obviously, if the Red Cross and the Salvation Army had not been able to shelter and feed so many people, the demands on the other, overloaded elements in the system would have been correspondingly greater. Thirdly, the total number of people made homeless by Hurricane Andrew in 1992 was in the 180,000–250,000 range—thus the number of Hurricane Katrina evacuees being sheltered by the Red Cross and the Salvation Army alone was at least 70 percent and perhaps as high as 95 percent of the *total* number of people made homeless by the worst storm to have hit the United States before the summer of 2005.

Hurricane Katrina also wreaked havoc on the infrastructure in the Gulf Coast. Focusing again on Louisiana because that was where the damage was most severe, well over a million households lost electricity. Despite the assistance of distant utilities such as Tampa Electric, the recovery effort was not as effective as it had been after Hurricane Andrew. Thus two weeks after the storm there were still 250,000 households without power[19] and six months after the storm there were still pockets of New Orleans where the electricity had not been restored. In addition, the storm interrupted phone service for 3 million people and almost half of the Gulf Coast radio and television stations were forced to stop broadcasting.[20]

By some estimates the cost of the damage that the storm caused was several times the cost of Hurricane Andrew's damage. The Congressional Budget Office has estimated that dollar value of property damage was almost three times the figure for Hurricane Andrew: $100 billion for Katrina, $35 billion for Andrew. There was, in addition, a loss of several hundred thousand jobs and $28–44 billion in lost business for the Gulf Coast firms that could not produce or sell their goods and services because of the storm.[21] Hurricane Katrina also caused serious damage to the buildings and equipment of the state and local governments. An interesting example of damage that also constrained the city of New Orleans' ability to respond after the storm involved the police department which lost a large number of vehicles to the storm. Some police cruisers were parked in underground garages to protect them from the wind; others were parked on overpasses to protect them from the floodwaters. As it turned out, the cars in the garage were flooded and the cars on the overpasses were damaged by the wind and then stranded in high water.[22]

State and municipal tax revenues were also decimated by the storm. Louisiana ordinarily raises about 60 percent of its revenue through sales taxes which, of course, dry up when local businesses cannot sell their goods and services. Although much of the effect may be temporary, as the rebuilding effort will generate economic activity that will eventually refill the sales tax stream, municipal governments may have a more lasting problem because most of their revenues are from property taxes on now-abandoned or destroyed real estate.[23] Even if the homes are eventually rebuilt or repaired, their assessed values will likely remain at lower levels than before the storm until such time as the memories of Katrina fade.

DISCONNECTS IN THE SYSTEM

Many critics of the federal role in Hurricane Katrina relief have asserted that the federal government was too slow to act and that disaster victims in Louisiana, Alabama, and Mississippi suffered unnecessarily as a result. In general, the critics make two specific points beyond criticizing the general level of effort at the White House and FEMA. One is that the Secretary of the Department of Homeland Security, Michael Chertoff, took too long to declare Hurricane Katrina an "incident of national significance" and to convene meetings of senior officials from the departments and agencies to launch the relief effort. The other point is that the senior FEMA officials, principally FEMA Director Michael Brown, in charge of coordinating federal relief efforts did not take the initiative, but instead waited for the states to articulate their needs, oblivious to the fact that for a crucial couple of days, the state and local governments in Louisiana were unable to assess the situation and determine exactly what the needs were. The latter criticism actually extends beyond FEMA, as the president has been blamed for appointing executives at the agency that did not have the necessary credentials and expertise. There is a reason why the criticisms of FEMA and the White House leaders sound familiar. They are the same points that were made after Hurricanes Hugo and Andrew.

With respect to the first point, the term "incident of national significance" is more than mere bureaucratese. According to the National Response Plan, when such an incident is declared by the Homeland Security Secretary, the federal agencies are authorized to begin response operations without waiting for requests from the government of the affected states. The National Response Plan is, as many of government master plans, a bit circuitous and muddled in articulating the criteria that would have to be met in order for a natural disaster to qualify as an incident of national significance.

The Plan's Glossary of Terms defines an incident of national significance as

> an actual or potential high-impact event that requires a coordinated and effective response by and appropriate combination of Federal, State, local, tribal, nongovernmental, and/or private-sector entities in order to save lives and minimize damage, and provide the basis for long-term community recovery and mitigation activities.[24]

A literal interpretation of this definition in the past two years alone would conceivably have resulted in Hurricanes Katrina, Rita, Dennis, Ivan, Jean, and Charley all being declared as incidents of national significance because each was high-impact and required a coordinated and effective response. The obvious conclusion is that the National Response Plan definition has never been and perhaps was never meant to be interpreted literally.

In fact, the more important definition is of another term, "catastrophic incident." This definition comes closer to defining the criteria that are actually used in determining whether an event is an incident of national significance. According to the Plan Glossary, a catastrophic incident is

> Any natural or manmade incident, including terrorism, that results in extraordinary levels of mass casualties, damage, or disruption severely affecting the population, infrastructure, environment, economy, national morale, and/or government functions. A catastrophic event could result in sustained national impacts over a prolonged period of time; almost immediately exceeds resources normally available to State, local, tribal, and private-sector authorities in the impacted area; and significantly interrupts governmental operations and emergency services to such an extent that national security could be threatened. *All catastrophic events are Incidents of National Significance.*[25] (Emphasis added.)

The logic of imbedding the criteria for a critical term only in the definition of another, less critical term is something that can be left to whoever has the thankless task of revising the National Response Plan, but what is clear is that Hurricane Katrina (and not the other major hurricanes of the past few years) meets the definition of a "catastrophic incident" and is, ipso facto, considered an incident of national significance.

It is undeniable that energizing the heads of all of the federal departments and agencies through a declaration of an incident of national significance and the convening of high level interagency meetings in Washington might very well have had a positive effect on the federal response. How could it not? Every student of bureaucracy knows that when the Department Secretary or Agency Administrator recognizes something as having high priority, things happen faster than they otherwise do. Indeed, the federal track record in previous major hurricanes, as described in the preceding chapters, ought to have suggested that high level intervention would be necessary at some point anyway.

But it is another matter altogether to infer, as the Government Accountability Office and Select Bipartisan Committee do, that had these steps been taken by the Secretary or directed by the White House the disaster relief system would have been much more successful in responding to Hurricane Katrina. There are, indeed, several reasons for doubting that an earlier declaration would have made more than a modest difference in terms of meeting the needs of disaster victims stranded in flooded neighborhoods, hospitals or the Superdome or in terms of initiating the rebuilding process. One reason is that substantial proactive steps had already been taken even without the declaration. As noted above, numerous medical and search and rescue teams were already on alert and huge volumes of relief supplies had been staged in the region by the evening of the 28th (the storm hit early on the 29th) and had in fact been loaded onto 700 trailer trucks for rapid distribution.[26]

Even if a declaration of an incident of national significance had been made in Washington during the hours before the storm hit, the levees would still have breached and New Orleans would still have flooded. The amount of federal supplies and personnel pre-positioned near the likely disaster zone would probably not have been substantially greater than they already were because there would simply not have been enough time between a last minute declaration and the storm's landfall to get the disaster relief equivalent of substantially more "boots on the ground" (twenty or thirty additional medical and rescue teams, hundreds of additional trucks loaded with relief supplies) into parts of adjoining states that were far enough away from the storm to be protected, but close enough to be able to get to New Orleans and other coastal communities quickly after the storm moved on.

A decision to sharply increase prepositioning two or three days before the storm's landfall would, of course, have allowed for more time for the supplies and personnel to be moved into position. However, such a large additional investment in prepositioning for a storm's whose severity and exact landfall were still uncertain would surely have seemed an overly expensive precaution to federal executives. In this regard it is worth recalling that much of the most severe damage was from post-storm flooding and the levee breaching which would likely not have been included in any declaration that was made before the storm hit. It is also worth noting that the city of New Orleans had not even ordered a mandatory evacuation until a day before landfall and the governor of Lousiana had not made any specific requests for additional pre-positioning help when she wrote to the president on Saturday, two days before landfall. Among other things, the governor's letter requested debris removal and direct FEMA grants to disaster victims[27]—things that would not be necessary until after the disaster. Furthermore, departments other than Homeland Security and Defense whose roles in disaster relief were secondary in comparison would have been especially concerned about over-investing in pre-positioning and Defense and Homeland Security (FEMA) may have felt that they were doing more than anyone else already. This is not to say that a declaration of national significance would have been unimportant. It could very well have accelerated some federal activity—but it would not have made a material difference to the amount of pre-positioned supplies and personnel and thus would not have dramatically improved the response effort during the first day or two after the storm. In any event, on the 29th the president issued a disaster declaration which, if the system had worked according to plan, ought to have given the federal coordinating officer all the authority he or she would need to direct other federal agencies to do what needed to be done to alleviate the suffering in New Orleans and nearby communities.

Of course, the system did not work according to plan and this is another reason to believe that the beneficial effects of a declaration of national significance have been overestimated. According to the National Response Plan, when an incident of national significance is also a declared disaster (which would usually be the case, according to the definition of a catastrophic incident and certainly was the case for Katrina), "federal support to states is delivered in accordance with the relevant provisions of the Stafford Act," (the Disaster Relief Act)[28] This means that the National Response Plan calls for the standard disaster relief procedure of relying upon states to articulate their need before federal resources are provided—even during catastrophic disasters/incidents of national significance.

As has been noted, the standard procedure works well when states and local governments are able to assess the disaster situation accurately, particularly during the early phases of the relief effort because that is when the needs of disaster victims are most dire. During the first day after Katrina made landfall, Louisiana and New Orleans did not have a clear picture of the situation and as a result were unable to decide how to best utilize their own resources, not to mention how to best use federal resources.

During the first day, in fact, there was substantial confusion about the situation with respect to the levees in New Orleans. This was due to the chaotic conditions and the loss of communications capabilities due to storm damage. Many first responders—the fire, police, and emergency management personnel whose role in the system is to appraise local conditions and forward situation reports up the line for consolidation with other local reports—lost their equipment, vehicles, and in some cases even buildings in the storm. State officials, therefore, knew only that the situation was bad, not where it was worst. And not where it was about to get worse— although given the fact that the levees had repeatedly been identified as major vulnerabilities, it was obvious that it would get worse all across the city if the levees failed.

Indeed on that first day it appeared for a very brief period that the storm had not been as bad as had been predicted. This was, of course, before it was understood that the levees had breached and when that happened it was the equivalent of a second catastrophic disaster in New Orleans. According to both the White House and Select Bipartisan Committee reports on the response to Hurricane Katrina, the status of the levees was unclear throughout the first day of the storm. There was a report as early as 9:12 a.m. on August 29 that there was at least one break in the levee system and that flooding had been observed. Later reports indicated that flooding had resulted from high water pouring over intact levees, which would obviously pose less of a threat to the city, and as late as 6 p.m. that day the White House was informed by federal disaster officials that the levees had not been breached.[29] FEMA Director Michael Brown, the federal coordinating officer in Louisiana, told a national television audience at 9 p.m. that night that there had "only" been some surges of water over the top of the levees, not breaches and the senior White House official on duty that night reportedly left the White House at 10 p.m. thinking that the levees had held.[30] The facts that there were hundreds of breaches and that soon 80 percent of New Orleans would be under water were not clear until the morning of August 30 and shortly thereafter Hurricane Katrina was designated as an incident of national significance and a declaration was issued by Secretary Chertoff.

The point in reviewing the time line with respect to the levee breaches is that even if the secretary had held the interagency meeting and issued the declaration sooner, the situation in New Orleans on the 29th would still have been unclear and the federal coordinating officer would still not know exactly what help the state needed. This is, of course, one reason why some observers have suggested that situation assessment in catastrophic disasters/catastrophic incidents/incidents of national significance should be federalized.

An earlier declaration by the Secretary of Homeland Security would also have done little to address the other main problems that have been identified by every post-Katrina study: officials at the federal and state levels who were not adequately trained for their roles in the relief effort, lack of understanding among federal officials of the National Response Plan, and the absence of the kind of detailed operational plans among the federal, state, and municipal agencies that were needed to support the National Response Plan.

In terms of the standards for measuring the success of a disaster relief operation, it is obviously clear that the relief effort in Hurricane Katrina was an abject failure in a number of respects, despite the huge number of personnel and supplies that were thrown into the fray. Large numbers of disaster victims in Louisiana were stranded in life-threatening situations for days in the Superdome and in flooded neighborhoods of New Orleans. Many went without urgently required medical care and tens of thousands were kept in inadequate shelter, without food and water for days. Further, electricity and water services were not restored quickly for hundreds of thousands of people.

THE LESSONS FROM KATRINA

A consensus finding in all the studies of the response to Hurricane Katrina was that critical information was not available to the key decision makers. The Select Bipartisan Committee in Congress referred to this as the "fog of war." The analogy captures the effect that lack of knowledge can have on decision makers, but it is otherwise misleading. The fog of war is at least partly deliberate, as it is the intended result of actions taken by adversaries (and sometimes even allies) to obscure the location of military forces and create uncertainty about their strategy, tactics and capabilities. Deliberate uncertainty could also be a factor in terrorist incidents when consequence managers need to consider whether an attack is diversionary or part of a series of attacks and whether there is a risk of a secondary attack at the initial site in which the first responders might be targeted (as has been the case in some terrorist incidents in Israel). Obviously, the uncertainty that impaired the response to Hurricane Katrina was something much different and in this context it makes more sense to recognize that the "fog of disaster relief" is a distinctly different phenomenon.

Just as uncertainty and information overload are inescapable features of war, they seem as well to have been inevitable in the responses to major relief operations. What has made them inevitable is, of course, the scale and geographical dispersion of the disaster itself and the complexity of the response system itself—with its too-numerous actors at the federal, state, and private sector levels—and the system has only grown in complexity after President Carter sought to consolidate functions at the federal level by establishing FEMA in 1979. Clearing the fog created by the complexity of the system will require more than flying squads of federal damage assessors or, alternatively, better communications gear and training for state and local damage assessors. Indeed, investments in better damage assessment techniques, more rugged communications equipment, and more extensive training were made after each of the major storms discussed in this book, yet the fog has obviously persisted.

Other lessons are that the state and local governments, particularly in Louisiana—the hardest-hit state, were not as well prepared as they should have been and that coordination among the federal departments was too cumbersome. As the third of the quotes offered at the beginning of the chapter indicated, these particular lessons had also been drawn in the post-mortems of Hurricanes Andrew and Hugo. Even more troubling, they are the same lessons that were drawn by the National Governors Association in 1978 and the Carter administration after Three Mile Island.

As the designated proprietor, so to speak, of the overall disaster relief system, FEMA has been assigned responsibility for ensuring that after each round of post-mortems there would be a renewed emphasis on preparedness at the state and local government levels and among the federal family of agencies. Unfortunately this emphasis seems to have had the staying power of the typical New Year's resolution—the commitment to preparedness has gradually slackened as the memories of a particular disaster grow less vivid and routine operations inexorably resume their priority over the attention of officials in every government agency at the federal and state level. Remarkably, this has even been true for FEMA, the agency with the greatest stake in preparedness and interagency coordination. Given the fact that preparedness has always ebbed in the months and years after events such as a major earthquake, hurricane, or terrorist event, there is no reason to expect anything different in the future as long as the existing structure of the disaster relief system remains intact. Some ideas for changing the system to place a greater emphasis on preparedness for catastrophic disasters will be offered in the concluding chapter.

A final lesson from Hurricane Katrina is that assertive presidential leadership again proved to be necessary to achieve unity of effort by the federal agencies. President Bush was, indeed, widely criticized for not having asserted himself sooner to remove whatever procedural or political hurdles were compromising the relief effort in the Gulf Coast. His delay is a major concern from the political perspective as it may have repercussions on the prospects of the Republican party in future elections, particularly in the Gulf Coast states and other disaster prone areas. However, from the perspective of the disaster relief system it is important to note that this White House's intervention was merely the latest in a series of presidential interventions that were required to set straight the federal response effort after catastrophic disasters.

As has been noted, in 1972 President Nixon took what was at the time the extraordinary step of sending the vice president on a fact-finding tour of the area affected by Hurricane Agnes, and in 1979 President Carter assigned a trusted White House staffer to coordinate policy toward Three Mile Island and appointed a special representative to be the White House's eyes and ears on scene. The first President Bush intervened after Hurricane Andrew in 1992 by appointing the Secretary of Transportation as a relief "tsar" after the federal relief effort came under heavy criticism. President Clinton did not wait for problems to emerge in the Midwest Floods of 1995 and held a flood relief summit to ensure that the federal agencies were responsive. Repeated presidential interventions in catastrophic disaster relief efforts clearly suggest that there is something in the water—some very basic flaw or flaws in the design of the system that has been repeatedly addressed on an ad hoc basis, but not fixed.

As suggested earlier, the complexity of the system is one flaw. Another is that at the federal level, the system is out of alignment. Whether it is an independent agency or part of a larger department, FEMA (or whatever a successor agency with the same portfolio might be called) is too politically weak for the authorities and capabilities that the government's plans for the infrequent catastrophic disasters and major terrorist incidents confer on it. For most disasters the issue over FEMA's authorities never comes into play because the only federal action is for FEMA alone to reimburse the affected state. In other disasters when the federal operational role is limited or are exercised in noncontroversial ways—for example, transporting relief supplies to a disaster scene with military aircraft—FEMA and the agencies it works with are not stressed by situational uncertainty or confusing information about the effects of the disaster because the state and local governments understand and are able to articulate their needs.

It has been argued since at least the National Academy of Public Administration study of FEMA after Hurricane Andrew in 1992 that the alignment problem should be fixed by institutionalizing direct presidential involvement in the response to catastrophic disasters, instead of relying upon ad hoc interventions. In effect, the idea is to assign FEMA a godfather in the White House—a senior political official, close to the president—who would be able to intervene during disasters to ensure that all of the federal agencies have the proper sense of urgency and priorities. That senior White House official could also put some teeth into the requirement that FEMA and the other agencies develop the operational plans envisioned by the National Response Plan, train their staffs for emergencies, and participate in exercises that realistically evaluate their response capabilities.

Before examining this and other recommendations, two other models for disaster relief systems will be described to provide a sense of design alternatives.

Chapter 7

TWO OTHER MODELS

As one would expect, the disaster relief systems in other countries differ considerably in capability and design from the system in the United States. For example, many countries in Africa and Central Asia have only rudimentary systems that entail little more reliance upon their military forces and help from the agencies of the United Nations and nongovernmental organizations such as the Red Cross and Catholic Relief Services. Military forces in these countries do many of the same things that military forces in the United States do during disasters—but the differences are that the civilian agencies of these governments have little or no operational capability and, in some countries, the principle of government safety nets for disadvantaged people is not as well developed. Thus disaster relief in many countries amounts to military forces transporting and distributing donated emergency supplies (food, water, blankets, tents, medicines) to disaster victims. Military personnel and equipment may also be used to dig people out from landslides, rescue individuals trapped inside collapsed buildings, construct temporary shelters, and provide emergency medical care to people injured in the disaster.

In terms of evaluating whether there are aspects of another country's system that could be adopted to improve the functioning of the disaster relief system in the United States, it obviously makes sense to compare apples to apples: countries that have economic and political structures that are similar to the United States. With respect to the political structure, the appropriate comparison is with other countries that have a federal-state structure and a disaster relief system that is not primarily military. The two most prominent points of comparison according to these standards are Canada and Australia. Despite their similar governmental structures, there are substantial differences between the U.S. disaster relief program and the Canadian and Australian programs.

For the purposes of this brief analysis, the broad features of the system in the United States will be summarized and then compared to the Australian and Canadian systems. The basic feature of the U.S. program is that the states have primary responsibility for attending to the safety and well-being of their residents, but states can request federal assistance which can be authorized only by the president and only for situations in which it has been determined that the disaster in some way overwhelmed the response capacity of the state. As has been observed earlier, this has led to politicization of decisions at the lower end of the disaster spectrum—that is to say that federal assistance has occasionally been authorized for situations where the disaster did not actually come anywhere near overwhelming the state. At the upper end of the spectrum the issue, of course, is completely different. For major emergencies there is virtual unanimity that federal assistance is warranted and the political issue is whether the system as a whole and the federal government, in particular, are doing enough, fast enough to meet the needs of disaster victims.

The general rule in the United States is that when a disaster is declared, the federal government will reimburse the affected state for most of its disaster relief expenditures for things like road clearance, reconstruction of public buildings, emergency feeding, and sheltering of disaster victims. If the disaster is severe enough the federal government may also provide operational assistance to the state and will defray most of the associated costs. The ordinary reimbursement rate is 75 percent for state expenditures. In addition, the federal government ordinarily also assumes 75 percent of its costs in providing operational assistance to the state. The receiving state would pay the remaining 25 percent. Under some circumstances the president may agree to reduce the state share of the cost of federal operational assistance to 10 percent or zero percent and correspondingly increase the federal share to 90 or 100 percent.

Above and beyond the general reimbursements funded by FEMA, other federal government agencies have their own emergency assistance programs that are funded entirely out of the federal budget. For example, FEMA provides cash grants and vouchers to families victimized by disaster; the Agriculture Department offers emergency food stamps to disaster victims, the Department of Labor operates a disaster unemployment insurance program for residents who lose their jobs due to the disaster, and the

Defense Department may cover the costs that the states incur when they utilize National Guard units in disaster relief.

The disaster relief agency in the United States has always been a civilian agency and it has gone through several incarnations in the past forty years. Early in the 1970s there were several disaster relief agencies, none of which were independent, stand-alone bureaucratic entities. In 1979, those agencies were merged into a single, independent agency, FEMA, that for a short period in the late 1990s was actually given Cabinet status. The agency lost Cabinet status when the Clinton administration left office in 1999 and since then FEMA has been swallowed up by a newly created agency, the Department of Homeland Security. One of the rationales for FEMA's merger into the Department of Homeland Security was that the disaster relief system was the backbone of the system that would be used to manage the consequences of a major terrorist attack. Indeed, the system was used as the basis for the government's management of the humanitarian consequences of the September 11, 2001, terrorist attacks in New York and Washington.

AUSTRALIA

Like the United States, Australia has a three-tired governmental structure for disaster relief. At the national level, Emergency Management Australia is the equivalent to FEMA and there are emergency management agencies and committees at the state/territory as well as at the local government levels. As is the case in the United States, Australian states and territories have the primary responsibility for providing for the safety of their citizens. However, Australian states and territories are, generally speaking, more powerful with respect to domestic affairs vis-à-vis the national government than states are in the United States. As a result the Australian federal government has a more limited role in providing operational assistance to the states/territories and when federal assets are committed to the relief effort they operate under the direction of the state/territory. In the United States, federal assets remain under federal command when they assist states in disaster relief. Moreover, when operational assistance is authorized by Canberra, a single federal agency is usually designated to provide it—without having to operate under the direction of Emergency Management Australia. Usually the single federal agency is the military. However, when more than one agency is involved, Emergency Management Australia would be responsible for coordinating their combined efforts.

Like FEMA, Emergency Management Australia is not an independent agency. Until 2001 it was part of the Department of Defence and it is now a subordinate organization within the Australian equivalent of the Department of Justice. (Despite being part of the Attorney-General's Department, Emergency Management Australia does not have a role in maintaining law and order.) Again like FEMA, Emergency Management Australia coordinates preparedness activities and acts as a clearinghouse for best practices in emergency management and disaster relief. A final similarity is that Emergency Management Australia's portfolio includes consequence management after terrorist events. Like FEMA, the agency is responsible for the overall preparedness of the nation (not just the federal agencies) for dealing with the humanitarian effects of terrorism—most of the victims in the 2002 terrorist bombing of the resort in Bali were Australians and this, plus observation of events in the United States and elsewhere, has sensibly heightened the country's emphasis on what it calls "counter-terrorism."

Despite these organizational similarities between Emergency Management Australia and FEMA, there are substantial differences between the Australian and American disaster relief programs. One is that Emergency Management Australia has no direct operational role in disaster relief—it does not provide grants or vouchers directly to disaster victims as FEMA does; nor does it set up centers where victims can go to apply for benefits. Those functions are the responsibility of the state and territory. Another and related difference is that Emergency Management Australia does not actually manage the process through which states and territories receive federal financial assistance; i.e., federal reimbursement for their disaster expenditures.

The Australian model separates the responsibility for preparedness and operational coordination from the responsibility for managing the reimbursement process. Emergency Management Australia is responsible for preparedness and may have a role in coordination during an emergency; the Department of Transport and Regional Services manages the money. In the United States, FEMA is responsible for preparedness, operational coordination, and money management. FEMA writes the checks that reimburse states, issues grants to individuals, transfers funds to other federal agencies to reimburse them for their disaster relief costs, and manages contracts with private sector vendors and nongovernment organizations. Judging from the reports about fraud and corruption associated with the response to Hurricane Katrina, it seems appropriate to wonder whether it is wise to expect one agency to be able to juggle both the financial management and operational coordination balls at the same time during the chaotic conditions of a major disaster or terrorist attack.

Perhaps the most important difference between the American and Australian program relates to the process through which the decision to authorize federal assistance is made. As has been noted, in the United States federal reimbursement of state disaster expenditures is made by FEMA only after it has been determined that the state has been overwhelmed in some respect by the effort of responding to a disaster. A formal determination is required and the determination must be made by the president. There is no equivalent in Australia to the presidential disaster declaration.

Australia's mechanism for reimbursing states and territories is known as the "Natural Disaster Relief Arrangements" which are, as noted, administered by the Department of Transport and Regional Services. Under the Natural Disaster Relief Arrangements, a state or territory receives reimbursement when its disaster relief expenditures on a given disaster exceed a preset level. In other words, the decision to authorize reimbursement is based upon objective criteria and is essentially automatic. It is also depoliticized.

By American standards the amount that triggers federal reimbursement is quite small—but then again in recent years Australia has incurred only about $3 billion in *annual* disaster damage.[1] Hurricane Katrina caused thirty times that much damage. Federal reimbursement is available for most of the same types of expenditures that qualify for reimbursement in the U.S. disaster relief program—basically the cost that the state/territory incurred in providing emergency food and shelter for victims and repairing public facilities damaged in the disaster.

Unlike the United States where the percentage of a state's disaster relief costs that the federal government reimburses (75, 90, or even 100%) is a political judgment, Australia's reimbursement is keyed to the financial strength of the state/territory. The Department of Transport and Regional Services reimburses 50 percent of a state/territory's eligible outlays over a set percentage (0.225%) of the state/territory's tax receipts. Seventy-five percent reimbursement kicks in when the outlays reach 0.35375 percent of tax revenues. Thus a state that had tax revenues of $100 million would not be reimbursed at all for disaster relief outlays that totaled less than $225,000. Half of the outlays above $225,000 and below $353,750 would be reimbursed. Seventy-five percent of the outlays in excess of $353,750 would be reimbursed.

Since the trigger points for 50 percent and 75 percent reimbursement are higher for the states/territories that collect the most taxes and assuming tax receipts are a reasonable proxy for the size of a state or territory's economy, Australia's reimbursement policy results in relatively lower reimbursement for wealthier states/territories and relatively higher reimbursement for the states/territories that are less well-off economically. An instructive analogy here would be Social Security benefits in the United States which offer more generous returns (as a percentage of the amount of Social Security taxes individuals pay) for low-wage earners than for high-wage earners. To some extent, the United States has occasionally sought to accomplish a similar income-adjustment through presidential decision to authorize 90 or 100 percent reimbursement for less well-off states; but that is a political judgment and the higher reimbursement rates have just as often been authorized for relatively wealthy states where there are upcoming elections. Moreover, 90 or 100 percent reimbursements amplify the incentives for states, local governments, and even individuals and private sector organizations to spend less on preparedness on the presumption that whatever the costs are of inadequately preparing for disasters, most if not all of them will ultimately be assumed by the federal government.

The phenomenon of federal "generosity" having the potentially negative effect of reducing the incentive for other elements in the system to invest as much as they should in preparedness will be discussed more fully in the next chapter. At this point it should be noted that according to Australia's Department of Transport and Regional Services, the phenomenon is of serious enough concern that

> a principal objective of the NDRA is to ensure that disaster relief assistance does not operate as a disincentive to effectively plan, mitigate and allocate sufficient resources for disasters or to discourage individuals or businesses taking out appropriate insurance to protect their assets and income.[2]

CANADA

More familiar to Americans, Canada's federal structure resembles Australia's, in that, its provinces are constitutionally as powerful as Australia's states and territories with respect to domestic affairs, including of course disaster relief. As a result, Canadian provinces also rely less upon federal assistance during disasters than do U.S. states. One indicator of this lower reliance is the fact that in the past thirty-five years the federal government of Canada has paid out less than $2 billion total in disaster assistance to the provinces. By way of comparison, FEMA spent more than twice as much as that on the relief effort in just one state, Mississippi, after Hurricane Katrina.[3]

Of course, another reason for the relatively small size of the Canadian program is the fact that Canada, like Australia, has been fortunate enough to not have to face natural disasters or terrorist attacks that are anywhere near as extensive or intensive as Hurricane Katrina, the September 11 attacks, or Hurricane Andrew. The main natural disasters in Canada are snow and ice storms, river floods, and forest fires.

The Canadian equivalent to FEMA is the Emergency Management and National Security Branch of Public Safety and Emergency Preparedness Canada (PSEPC) which was established as a ministerial department (the equivalent of a Cabinet-level department in the United States) in 2004 and is the equivalent of the U.S. Department of Homeland Security. Also incorporated into PSEPC are the Canadian Border Service, the Royal Canadian Mounted Police, the Canadian Security Intelligence Service and the Correctional Service Canada.

As a result of the predominance of law enforcement and intelligence functions in PSEPC, it is fair to say that the disaster relief is a secondary priority of the department. This is not a new phenomenon. Even before the establishment of PSEPC, the FEMA-equivalent was the Office of Critical Infrastructure Protection and Emergency Preparedness which was part of the now-defunct Department of Public Safety and Emergency Preparedness and prior to that its predecessor—once-removed agency—Emergency Preparedness Canada, was part of the Department of National Defence. Canada's policies toward the federal role in disaster relief help explain why the federal disaster relief agency has traditionally been given secondary status in the Canadian bureaucracy.

As is the case in Australia, there is no requirement for an explicit disaster declaration by the Canadian prime minister and the decision to authorize federal reimbursement is essentially automatic. The trigger, however, is not a sliding scale based on tax receipts but is instead based on per capita disaster relief expenditures by the province. After a province expends more than $1 per capita in disaster relief, or after PSEPC and the province agree that per capita expenditures are very likely to exceed $1 per capita, federal reimbursement is authorized according to Canada's Disaster Financial Assistance Arrangements.

Like Australia's Natural Disaster Relief Arrangements, Canada's Disaster Financial Assistance Arrangements are essentially a cost-sharing formula that determines exactly how much of the province's disaster relief expenditures will be reimbursed by the national government. As is the case in Australia, there is no reimbursement for provincial relief expenditures below a predetermined level ($1 per capita for the Canadian province, 0.225% of the Australian state's tax revenue). Thus a province with three million people would receive no reimbursement from the national government of Canada if its relief expenditures for a particular disaster were $3 million or less.

Once the $1 per capita figure is exceeded, reimbursement is available, and the rate of reimbursement increases as per capita spending increases. Canada reimburses provincial disaster relief expenditures according to the following scale:

Up to $1 per capita	Zero
$1 to $3 per capita	50%
$3 to $5 per capita	75%
Over $5 per capita	90%[4]

There is no ceiling on reimbursement, as provinces may spend what they want in disaster relief, but only certain types of relief expenditures are eligible for reimbursement. This is also similar to the reimbursement guidelines in Australia. Both countries limit reimbursement to the costs of emergency food and shelter and repairing public facilities damaged in a disaster. Canada also reimburses provincial payments that cover the uninsured losses of homeowners—excluding vacation homes. Like Emergency Management Australia, PSEPC does not directly provide cash grants and vouchers to disaster victims and whatever centers that might be set up for disaster victims to apply for government benefits are the responsibility of the province.

The Disaster Financial Assistance Arrangements are intended to serve the same objective as Australia's Natural Disaster Relief Arrangements: maintaining incentives for the provinces to shoulder the burden of disaster preparedness and cost-conscious management of the response effort. In both countries, the incentive is provided by reimbursement rates that are not as high as they are in the United States.

The national government of Canada may also provide direct operational assistance to the relief effort in a province. Ordinarily this assistance would be by the military or Health Canada, the equivalent of the U.S. Department of Health and Human Services, which has some medical response capabilities.[5] The minister of PSEPC would be the coordinator of the federal operational support to the province but the federal assets would be under the direction of the provincial government as long as they were engaged in the relief effort.

The most extensive use of military forces for disaster relief in Canada was during the ice storms of January 4–8, 1998, which knocked out power to a million homes with four million occupants. Three provinces (Quebec, Ontario, and New Brunswick) requested military aid on the third day of the storm because ice-covered roads were blocked by downed trees and power lines and people in outlying districts were stranded without power and access to supplies. *Operation Recuperation* involved more than 15,000 soldiers who spent several weeks rescuing people, clearing roads, distributing generators, fuel, and food. The forces were also used to maintain law and order in the city of Montreal.[6] In Canada there is no equivalent to the

Posse Comitatus law in the United States, so Canadian military forces can be used in law enforcement at the request of a province.

OBSERVATIONS

For a variety of reasons (greater population density, more intensive economic development, and the nature of the disasters) the consequences of disasters in the United States have been much greater than in Canada and Australia. There are, nevertheless, many similarities between the disaster relief programs in each country. Each country's program reflects its basic constitutional structure in assigning primary responsibility for disaster relief and consequence management to the state or province. Each country has a civilian disaster relief agency at the federal level to orchestrate national preparedness for disasters and for terrorist events and each government provides a federal helping hand to the state/territory/province when it is faced with an emergency without actually assuming primary responsibility for disaster relief. Only in the United States does the federal agency responsible for preparedness also have direct operational responsibilities above and beyond coordinating federal relief activities during major disasters.

Canada and Australia seek to achieve the balance between supplementing and substituting for state-provincial governments by putting the state or province unambiguously in charge of relief operations and by limiting the amount that the federal government will reimburse. In the United States, the federal government has traditionally had a more direct role in domestic affairs and in disaster relief in particular, so the option of putting a state in unambiguous charge of the entire range of relief operations may not be practical; but the option of adopting something like the Australian or Canadian financial arrangements is. There are two aspects to the financial arrangements that deserve note. One is different reimbursement rates; the other is the depoliticization of the process for deciding which disasters warrant federal assistance and which ones don't.

To illustrate the differences in reimbursement, consider the following example. If a state in the United States experiences a disaster that is severe enough for federal assistance, it can expect to be reimbursed at a minimum rate of 75 percent for its eligible disaster relief expenditures. Under some circumstances the state could be reimbursed at a 90 or 100 percent rate. (For the sake of this example, it is assumed that all of the expenditures are eligible for reimbursement; e.g., they are not routine, nondisaster expenditures that are mistakenly categorized as disaster relief.) Thus if that state spent $100 million in disaster relief, it would eventually get $75 million (or perhaps even $90 or $100 million) back from the federal government. Assuming that the same state had a population of 10 million and that Canada's reimbursement rules were applied, the state would get a maximum federal payment of $70 million.* There would be negligible difference in the rate of reimbursement between the American and Australian systems because the trigger for 75 percent reimbursement in Australia is so low (about one-third of 1%). If a significantly higher percentage of tax revenue was used as the trigger, as arguably it should, given the size of some state budgets in the United States, the result would be lower reimbursement to the states than under the current system. Lower reimbursement rates are an important consideration. Not only do they restrain federal spending, they give a stronger incentive for states to take emergency preparedness seriously because that helps reduce costs and to manage their disaster relief expenditures carefully.

In the United States declaring a disaster is inherently a political process—this is not to say that all disaster declarations are politically or politically controversial. In fact, the opposite is true. The vast majority of disaster declarations are noncontroversial and the only ones that are controversial are the least important disasters—the events that cause relatively little damage and appear not to actually have overwhelmed the response capability of the affected state. The declarations are political in the sense that they are based on the judgment of politicians who have been elected (the president) or appointed (the FEMA director) and who do not have objective, universally accepted criteria upon which to base their judgments.

The opposite is true in Canada and Australia where there are objective, long-standing criteria that are applied without having to secure a formal decision by the head of an agency or of the government. This is important in a few respects. Timing is not one of them. The path for securing a presidential decision about a disaster is smooth and well-worn. Presidents get requests from the governors and advice from the FEMA directors in a matter of hours, and when conditions are urgent can issue disaster declarations virtually while the rain is still falling, the high winds are still blowing, or the ground is still shaking from post-quake tremors.

What is important is that the process is not as well-aligned with under-lying constitutional assumptions as the Canadian and Australian processes are. The primary responsibility for disaster relief in Canada, the United

---

* In this example, under the Canadian system, the province would get nothing for the first $10 million and then only 50 percent of the next $10 million. Thus for the first $20 million it spent, it would get $5 million in reimbursement. In the U.S system the reimbursement for the first $20 million would be $15 million. At higher per capita expenditure levels, the Canadian rate accelerates and the difference between the U.S. rate narrows, as long as the standard 75 percent rate continues to apply in the United States.

States, and Australia belongs, as has been repeatedly noted, to the state or provincial level of government. Canada and Australia recognize this by making federal funding available automatically based upon the actions of the state or province. Once the state or province spends a certain amount, it is eligible for reimbursement according to a predetermined scale. There is no second-guessing of the decision of the state/province to provide disaster relief at a certain level to its residents, although there are post-facto audits to ensure that eligible expenditures are the only ones that are being reimbursed.

In the United States, the state governor must submit a formal request to the federal government, which is supposed to justify its request for assistance. According to FEMA guidelines, the justification should include an estimate of the damage from the disaster and an explanation of "the nature and amount of State and local resources that have been or will be committed to alleviating the results of the disaster."[7] The legislation upon which these vague guidelines are based clearly connotes concern on the part of Congress that enterprising state governments will request federal assistance even when they do not really need it, in order to ease their own budget pressures. Indeed, this concern is not without reason as every year there are a handful of state requests that are turned down because the disaster is not severe enough to merit federal assistance and, as has been noted, some not-so-severe disasters are occasionally approved for federal assistance.

For major hurricanes, earthquakes, flood, and other disasters the review process is somewhat perfunctory in that the federal government knows as well as the state that the damage will be extensive. This is certainly the case for catastrophic disasters where the declaration is issued within hours— well before anyone, even a federal flying squad of situation assessors, could have completed a credible assessment of the damage and the needs of the victims.

In effect, with respect to the major disasters, the ones that account for the vast majority of federal disaster relief expenditures, the U.S. disaster declaration process is perfunctory and serves no practical purpose. All of the participants in the process (the state emergency management agency, the governor, FEMA, and the president) agree that the states need help in responding to the "big ones," and for the "really big ones" the federal government issues the declaration without even waiting for the documentation it would require before evaluating requests for help in "small ones." It is, in fact, only the "small ones" for which the review process makes any sense at all, even though the federal government's stakes are generally insignificant, relative to the financial and physical stakes in disasters like Hurricanes Katrina and Andrew and even noncatastrophic disasters such as Hurricanes Jeanne and Ivan in 2004 which concentrated their damage in Florida but also affected Georgia and some other states.

This point will be returned to in the final chapter. Not only is the disaster declaration process inconsistent with the states having primary responsibility for disaster relief, but it also has the untoward effect of misdirecting some of the intellectual energies of the federal government toward the disasters where the stakes are the lowest. An automatic process analogous to Canadian or Australian system makes more sense. It would release the federal government from having to involve itself in minor emergencies and allow it to concentrate on preparedness for major disasters. Under the current system in the United States, there is, in effect, a presumption that state governments cannot be trusted and, as we have seen, there have been instances in which states have managed to secure federal reimbursement for relatively minor disasters and a small number of state requests for federal assistance are in fact turned down each year.

However, if the declaration process were scrapped in favor of an automatic trigger as in Canada and Australia—what management guru Peter Drucker calls "creative abandonment"—the federal government would be able to get out of the business of second-guessing states in the fifty or sixty routine disasters that occur in the average year. If the right trigger were established, as it appears to have been in Canada, states would always have the financial incentive to manage relief operations effectively because their share of the costs would never get as low as it does in the United States. Further, since there is no federal reimbursement for disaster expenditures below the trigger level, the provinces always had to have paid what amounts to earnest money before federal aid could become available. Once a U.S. state has committed its earnest money in relief expendititures, there should be no reason for the federal government to determine for itself that the disaster meets some ill-defined standard. The automatic reimbursement approach would, moreover, be consistent with the premise that states have the primary responsibility for disaster relief and would result in equal treatment for all states regardless of the political clout of their delegations in Congress or their importance in an upcoming election.

Exactly what the automatic trigger might be warrants some study as the trigger in Canada might be too high and the trigger in Australia too low. For example, a $1 per capita trigger in California would mean that the state would have to spend $36 million on a single disaster before becoming eligible for federal assistance. Florida would have to spend $17 million on each disaster and in some years, the state has multiple disasters each of which would—under the Canadian approach—have separate $17 million triggers. In 2004 there were four disasters declared in Florida and two in California.

It should be noted again that adopting an automatic trigger keyed to the state's own expenditures will have no direct effect on the federal response to catastrophic disasters. With a Hurricane Katrina or Andrew there would be no doubt that relief expenditiures will quickly pass the trigger level and that various forms of federal operational support would be required. However, if the federal government were to get out of the business of responding to routine disasters, it would be better able to concentrate on addressing the shortcomings in preparedness that have been identified after each of the catastrophic disasters since 1972.

Chapter 8

CONCLUSION AND RECOMMENDATIONS

Despite its highly publicized shortcomings after several major hurricanes and the very strong criticism it has received in recent months from the Congress and the media, there is actually much to admire in the disaster relief system of the United States. Before discussing the various ideas that have been bruited about reforming the system, the strengths of the system ought to be acknowledged.

As long as all of the elements in the system are functioning—as they reliably do in all but the most severe emergencies—the disaster relief system has proven that it is capable of extraordinary accomplishments. In all but a few cases, the disaster relief system almost immediately provides disaster and terrorism victims with shelter, food, and medical care. Generally, all victims are able to apply for financial assistance from government agencies and insurance sources without much inconvenience or delay. Further, the process of repairing damage to homes, businesses, and public facilties typically begins as soon as the waters recede, the high winds stop howling, or the ground stops shaking. There were, to be sure, things that could have been done better in the response to the September 11 terrorist attacks, the Oklahoma City bombing, and the various major earthquakes and river floods that have affected the nation, but in each of these stressful situations the system has functioned reasonably well.

In each of these instances and numerous others, the system has demonstrated the ability to transport on short notice astonishingly large volumes of relief supplies from all over the country to a disaster zone. It has also been able to quickly distribute those supplies to disaster victims and simultaneously issue cash payments and vouchers that disaster victims can use to acquire medicine, clothing, food, and shelter. Admittedly, the steps that have sometimes been taken to accelerate the "retail" distribution of supplies and issue grants/vouchers to disaster victims have occasionally lowered the program's safeguards against fraud and abuse. The erroneous payments that result should not be discounted as merely the unavoidable costs of doing business in chaotic environments; but neither should they be taken to mean that the program as a whole is hopelessly lax in terms of its accountability to taxpayers and to the donors who contribute to the Red Cross and other nongovernment providers of relief. The fraud and abuse that occurs is small relative to the overall costs and is, in any event, offset at least to some extent by the program's auditing mechanisms to recapture fraudulent payments after the disaster response operation has wound down.

Another highly positive feature of the system—at all levels—is its remarkable ability to mobilize and deploy large numbers of highly capable response personnel. As has been noted earlier, most local governments have mutual aid agreements with the governments of neighboring communities to lend each other fire-fighting and law-enforcement assets during emergencies and most states have emergency management assistance compacts with other states to share National Guard and other emergency personnel during emergencies. As was noted in the discussion of Hurricane Katrina, National Guard troops from all over the country provided assistance to the Gulf Coast states. In fact, by the fifth day after the storm hit, there were almost as many Guard troopers from other states in Louisiana as there were Louisiana Guardsmen and by the sixth day the "other state" contingents were almost twice as large. Private sector corporations, notably utility companies, have similar arrangements with each other. Thus utility companies in other states—often other states that are far away from the scene of a disaster or terrorist event—routinely send emergency repair crews to help restore power and communications in disaster-stricken states and the deployments take place remarkably quickly as was illustrated in the power industry's response to Hurricane Andrew. That it had taken so long for the power to be restored in Louisiana after Hurricane Katrina reflects the damage that the storm caused to the utility infrastructure there, not any failing on the part of industry to lend a hand. Insurance companies dispatch extra claims personnel to disaster zones and the Red Cross and other nongovernmental organizations mobilize large numbers of volunteers from all over the country.

To be sure, all of these things occur with strong federal encouragement. FEMA, for example, has long promoted emergency management compacts among states. FEMA and its counterpart agencies at the state level have also long encouraged the formalization of mutual aid agreements among neighboring municipalities. Most adjoining cities and towns have, of course, always cooperated with each other when a disaster strikes, but as municipal governments have grown in terms of capabilities and complexity (e.g., new agencies, new technologies, new laws and regulations governing the execution of municipal functions) so too has the need for pre-arranged and formalized sharing agreements. The concept of the emergency management assistance compact actually evolved as a system improvement after Hurricane Andrew when it became clear that states would be unwise to rely too heavily upon federal assistance during the early stages of a response to a catastrophic disaster. Southern states initiated the sharing agreements and since 1993 FEMA and the U.S. Congress have encouraged expansion of the program to include every state. In 1996 Congress passed legislation that "consented" to states entering into such compacts with each other. Since legislation was not required in any event, the purpose of the legislation was two-fold: to encourage states to do more to fend for themselves and to prevent the states from preempting the president's right to federalize the National Guard through disaster relief commitments to other states.[1] Importantly, mutual aid and emergency management compacts do not depend upon a presidential disaster declaration or any other form of the federal authorization. Nor do they require operational direction by the federal coordinating officer or any other federal entity. From the federal perspective, once these agreements and compacts are negotiated, the sharing of resources during an emergency happens more or less automatically and this is how it should be.

Care should be taken in any reform efforts to ensure that these aspects of the system at the state/local government and private sector levels are maintained and even strengthened. One of the surest ways to weaken the self-organizing features of response in the private sector and at the state and local government level would be for the federal government to assume a more direct role in managing disaster responses. The very last thing that the federal government should do is crowd initiative at nonfederal levels out of the system in the name of improving the federal response to catastrophic disasters. Yet this is very likely what the outcome could be if care is not taken.

There are, obviously, aspects of the system that are less impressive and not all of them have to do with catastrophic disasters. One aspect is the phenomenon of "free riding" by private citizens and state/local governments. Free riding occurs when individuals or governments take advantage of the investment of others in public goods by reducing their own investment. Even though the free rider underinvests or choses not to invest at all, he is able to benefit from the public good—for example, federal disaster relief or military defense against a common enemy—while preserving investment funds for other purposes. Individual home owners free ride on the federal disaster relief program when they drop their flood or earthquake insurance policies in the expectation that damage to their homes in a storm or earthquake will be covered by disaster relief from the federal government. Further the very existence of federal disaster relief encourages some people to build (or rebuild) houses or business establishments in low-lying areas near rivers or on the beach in coastal communities where they are more likely to experience damage from storms than in inland locations. Obviously, when storms hit such areas, they cause considerably more damage than they would have if homes and business establishments had not been built there and the river banks and shorelines had remained undeveloped.

FREE RIDING AND OVERPROMISING

Free-ridership is not unique to the private sector. State and local governments free ride if and when they choose to underinvest in disaster preparedness on the unspoken assumption that the federal government will bail them out when disaster strikes. The fact is, of course, that such an assumption on the part of the states has historically proven to be a good bet as no congressional delegation would allow disaster relief to be withheld from their state even though the state government's inattention to preparedness could well have made the needs of disaster victims worse. In effect, the more effective and proactive the federal government becomes at providing disaster relief and the more generous it is in reimbursing state/local governments, the more it may be encouraging the states to trim their investments in preparedness.

In other words, under certain circumstances the federal element of the disaster relief program inadvertently encourages behavior that makes disaster relief more expensive and exposes more people to physical danger certainly from natural disasters and possibly from terrorist attacks. More proactive and generous federal involvement in disaster relief—in fact, even the perception that the federal government is proactive and generous— leads other elements in the system to "normalize" risk. That is to say that over time, basically every year that passes without a disaster that directly affects them, or every year in which there is active federal involvement in disasters elsewhere, individual families and business people and state/local governments increasingly act as if they assumed that the risk of sustaining unreimbursed damages is diminished. Families adjust to their perception of lowered risk, for example, by building (or rebuilding) vacation homes on the beach on the assumption that they will be able to avoid most of the financial cost of the next disaster which may not, in any event, arrive while they own that building. Local governments adjust to the perception of lower risk by relaxing rules about beachfront construction and by gradually reducing their emergency preparedness budgets in the years after "the big one" as both citizens and legislators inevitably focus more and more on the immediate concerns associated with the routine, daily functions of government such as running the schools, collecting the trash, managing the water system, and providing police and fire services to the community.

These adverse effects on disaster programs are, to some extent, inescapable given the incentives in the economy (e.g., income tax deductions for mortgages on primary and vacation homes, subsidized federal flood insurance, local promotion of economic development in resort communities) but the more active the federal government becomes, the more pronounced these effects will become.

Like each of the operational problems observed in this book, the dysfunctional process of inadvertently encouraging behavior that makes disasters worse is far from new. Neither is it newly discovered. As far back as 1973—six years before FEMA was germinated in the Carter administration laboratory—the Nixon White House issued a paper that called federal disaster assistance "so generous that individuals, businesses, and communities had little incentive to take initiatives to reduce personal and local hazards." Twenty-two years later in 1995 a "Bipartisan Natural Disaster Task Force" of the House reiterated the point with respect to communities and state governments.[2] Based on what happened in New Orleans in Hurricane Katrina, it seems clear that the preparedness incentives were not strong enough. Indeed, except during the immediate aftermath of a major disaster when the press and the public are attuned to the things that should be done to prevent the next disaster from being as bad, state and local governments, families and businesses always underinvest in preparedness at least in part because of their expectation that federal disaster assistance will compensate them for much of their losses.

The marketing that FEMA undertook during the Clinton administration to improve the agency's image and boost the morale of its employees—both worthy causes—likely enhanced these effects by implicitly and, presumably inadvertently, creating the impression that the agency had more capability than it had and creating political expectations that no single federal agency could fulfill during a hurricane like Katrina, Andrew, or Hugo.

The distribution of FEMA tee-shirts, jackets, and baseball caps to first responders that was referred to earlier is one example. As television stations broadcast news coverage of disasters, viewers saw pictures of first responders wearing FEMA gear and undoubtedly got the mistaken impression that it was FEMA personnel who were crawling into partially collapsed buildings looking for trapped survivors and providing on-scene medical triage and emergency medical support for injured people. The reality was, however, that the search and rescue teams were actually municipal firefighters from places like Dade County, Florida, or Arlington, Virginia, and the emergency medical personnel and physicians were from teams that had been assembled from volunteers at state health agencies, university hospitals, private group practices, the military, and the federal Public Health Service and Veterans Administration. Federal funds were used to purchase the specialized equipment that the search and rescue and medical teams needed, to defray the cost of their training, and to pay team member salaries during the relief operation—but the personnel and their capabilities did not reside at FEMA, even though the televised pictures suggested otherwise.

Interestingly, FEMA press releases still occasionally pin the FEMA label on actions of other organizations. For example, a February 1, 2006, press release on the Hurricane Katrina response highlights the accomplishments of the "FEMA Disaster Medical Assistance Teams" and "FEMA's Blue Roof program." The latter is, as the text of the press release conceded, actually a U.S. Army Corps of Engineers program under which blue plastic tarpaulins are fastened on damaged roofs so that families can continue to reside there while repairs are underway. The former are, as noted in the previous paragraph, composed of volunteers from everywhere but FEMA.[3]

Another effective marketing technique was the photo opportunities in which the FEMA director stood side by side with his equivalent at the state level and proclaimed that FEMA and the state were working as partners in the disaster relief operation. The word partner has many meanings. A partner can be a spouse with whom there is a lifetime commitment or an individual (or organization) with whom there is a formal contractual relationship for a limited purpose such as might exist between the co-owners of a business. A partner could also be an individual or organization with which there is only temporary cooperation, as with a dancing partner or a partner in crime. Of course, federal and state governments cooperate with each other all the time—in the language of the disaster relief system, from the early stages of preparedness in the years and months before disaster or terrorism strikes to the post-disaster reconstruction, but the second definition is the one that most closely approximates the relationship that is supposed to exist between the federal and state governments in the disaster relief program. However the contractual relationship is not one of equality. It is instead analogous to the limited partnerships that two corporations might form to take advantage of a business opportunity. The general partner is the corporation that is directly responsible for managing the business' daily operations and the corporation that is the limited partner is often only responsible for a limited range of functions, for example, financing or research and development. When the business is responding to a disaster in a state, the state government is the general partner and the federal government is the limited partner. The Disaster Relief Act and the traditions of the program clearly assign primary responsibility to the state, not co-responsibility to the federal and state governments or federal primary responsibility. The federal government, in the person of FEMA, is the general partner when the business is ensuring that all of the pieces in the overall disaster relief system fit together before disasters strike. The Carter administration recognized that a general partner was needed to orchestrate the overall system's preparedness—yet inadequate preparedness has been continued to be a major shortcoming, as the postmortem reports after Hurricanes Hugo, Andrew, and Katrina make clear.

Clearly, Hurricane Katrina ought to have disabused Congress, the media, and the public of whatever false confidence it might have had in FEMA after the 1990s, but criticisms of the agency imply that when FEMA is "fixed" or replaced by a more capable organization (as a May 2006 report by the Senate Committee on Homeland Security and Governmental Affairs recommended[4]), the disaster relief system will then be able to satisfy expectations for rapid and effective relief after catastrophic disasters or major terrorist events. As a result, the political furor in Washington over the inadequacy of the response to Hurricane Katrina will very likely only worsen the problem of unrealistic expectations in the future. The public will undoubtedly assume that once the Congress and the White House finish reforming or replacing FEMA the stage will be set for a more effective response to the next catastrophic hurricane or other disaster. It hardly needs to be said, but this was also the expectation after Three Mile Island and Hurricanes Hugo and Andrew.

The reality is, as all of the reports on Hurricane Katrina have acknowledged, that there were multiple points of failure, just as there were multiple points of failure after the other catastrophic disasters reviewed in this book. Fixating on the points of *operational* failure at the federal level will do little to address the points of failure in other elements of the system. Addressing FEMA's responsibility as the general partner for the overall capabilities of the disaster relief system makes more sense—but proposals for a reformed FEMA or a successor agency with exactly the same portfolio of functions and similar bureaucratic status do not address the reasons why the general partner function has not been and is not being effectively performed.

FEDERAL PREEMPTION OF STATES

The argument has been made by the Government Accountability Office (GAO) among others that catastrophic disasters such as Hurricane Katrina and Hurricanes Andrew, Hugo, and Agnes are simply different than "routine" disasters and thus that the federal government's role in disaster relief should be different than it is in the typical disaster. In a catastrophic disaster the federal government should, according to the GAO become the primary responder. For example in a 1993 report to Congress, GAO concluded that

> The federal strategy for responding to catastrophic disasters is deficient because it lacks provisions for the federal government to *immediately* (1) assess in a comprehensive manner the damage and the corresponding needs of disaster victims and (2) provide food, shelter, and other essential services when the needs of disaster victims outstrip the resources of the state, local, and private voluntary community.[5] [Emphasis added.]

Thirteen years later after Hurricane Katrina, GAO made the same point—that in catastrophic disasters "business as usual" protocols should be short-circuited and that the federal government should preempt the affected state government by assuming primary responsibility for disaster relief. In a February 2006 report to Congress, GAO faulted FEMA and its parent agency, the Department of Homeland Security, for "wait[ing] for the affected states to request assistance."[6] That is, for not preempting the state government.

Recommendations that the federal government preempt the states and assume primary responsibility in catastrophic disasters go both too far and not far enough. They go too far in the sense that a more active, indeed proactive federal role in disaster relief would exacerbate the free rider problem by suggesting to states, local governments, nongovernment organizations, and perhaps families that the federal "cavalry" that Kate Hale called for during Hurricane Andrew will be poised like a military strike force on the horizon to blitzkrieg to the rescue just as the next major disaster strikes and consequently that they can scale back their own investments in preparedness for unusually severe disasters or terrorist events. The recommendation goes too far as well in that it is inconsistent with the basic federal-state division of responsibilities under which disaster relief and other federal-state programs operate. This is, obviously, not an insurmountable problem—indeed there already are provisions for federal preemption even in the disaster relief program. In effect the federal government takes the lead in assessing the situation in chemical and biological incidents and assumes direct control over the law enforcement aspects of terrorist incidents that occur in states. However, expanding preemption to include response to natural catastrophic disasters will very likely encourage states and their representatives in Congress to push for ever more expansive criteria for distinguishing between truly catastrophic disasters and other storms. If the GAO recommendation were accepted, the federal government would eventually inherit the lead responsibility for responding to most major disasters, not just the catastrophic events that have tended to occur—like Hurricanes Hugo, Andrew, and Katrina—only once every five or ten years.

There is another negative consequence as well. Even though GAO and others argue that catastrophic disasters are different, the fact is that there are substantial similarities in relief operations after catastrophic disasters and all other disasters. This is particularly true of the private sector and the local government levels where most of the functions are actually identical. For example, the following functions will be performed by local officials in any disaster or terrorist incident:

Assessing the local situation,

Reporting information needed by state and federal officials,

Providing emergency information to the local population,

Mobilizing first responder personnel,

Prioritizing the use of rescue vehicles and ambulances,

Distributing relief commodities (food, water, blankets),

Managing traffic, and

Coordinating with mutual aid partners.

It would be a serious mistake to adopt any policy on the assumption that such functions would become less important once the federal government has taken over a relief operation. Yet this is exactly what advocates of federal preemption appear to believe. Further, the expectation that the federal government will begin to take over primary responsibility for disaster relief could very well lead to less emphasis on these disaster relief functions in state and local government budgets which would undoubtedly compromise the capability of the overall system.

An instructive analogy regarding another of the negative consequences of preemption is the disaster declaration process itself. Just as the definition of how serious a disaster must be to warrant a decision by the president to issue a disaster declaration and thus open the spigot of federal financial assistance is obviously blurred by politics at the low end of the spectrum of severity—witness the declaration of disasters after snowstorms in northern states—so too will the criteria for the designation of a catastrophic disaster be inevitably watered down in practice. In truth, the distinction between catastrophic disasters and other major disasters is necessarily both artificial and complex. Judgment is required, but judgment in the political environment inhabited by the disaster relief system will be influenced by pressures from governors, congressional delegations, and the media. Whoever ultimately has the responsibility for determining which disasters are catastrophic will be in the impossible position of justifying why one disaster merited federal preemption and another one did not. The result will be to lower the bar over time. As the federal government preempts the states in more and more disaster responses, the result will be the displacement of the very things that make the system work most of the time—state, local, and private sector preparedness and initiative.

The recommendation for federal preemption in catastrophic disasters does not go far enough in the sense that it would leave the federal responsibility for "routine" and catastrophic disasters in the same department or agency. Judging from the history of federal responses to catastrophic hurricanes, this may well only perpetuate the problem of inadequate response to catastrophic disasters.

1972	Hurricane Agnes
1989	Hurricane Hugo
1992	Hurricane Andrew
2001	Attacks on World Trade Center/Pentagon
2005	Hurricane Katrina

During the span of thirty-five years in which these five unarguably catastrophic events occurred, approximately 1,300 disasters were declared by the president. Two related points should be made about these statistics. One is that catastrophic disasters are a very tiny percentage of the disasters for which federal assistance is authorized. In most years "only" non-catastrophic disasters occur. The second point is that non-catastrophic disasters are obviously the routine business of FEMA and that is what the agency and the system it superintendents do well. This means that unless the basic system is changed, FEMA or whatever agency might take its place in the future will spend by far the vast majority of its time with what GAO calls "business as usual." Indeed, Congress and GAO will accentuate that emphasis, as they have in the past, by overseeing how effectively and efficiently the federal government responds to the business-as-usual disasters. State governors and state agencies will also be more concerned about how well FEMA performs with business-as-usual disasters because that is what will affect them most of the time.

This will be especially true for the elected officials from and in states that have not ever experienced a disaster or terrorist event that might be considered catastrophic. In fact, the number of states that have experienced catastrophic hurricanes in the thirty-five years is quite small (Louisiana, Florida, South Carolina, Pennsylvania, and the territory of Puerto Rico) and is likely to stay small unless global weather patterns shift. Catastrophic earthquakes are certainly conceivable in California and the New Madrid fault in the central United States, but the evidence suggests that the disaster relief system responds more effectively to earthquakes and that federal preemption in this area would serve no constructive purpose.

The result is that as long as the responsibility for routine and catastrophic disasters remains in FEMA or a successor agency, the habits and protocols that the agency learns and repeatedly relearns during the course of responding to the forty to sixty disasters that are declared in a typical year will necessarily dominate its culture and influence how it responds to atypical disasters. This is, in fact, what has been happening since before Hurricane Agnes in 1972. It will happen again in the future as the lessons of Hurricane Katrina fade, as they must.

Students of bureaucratic behavior and organizational culture know that organizations do not readily jettison the habits and protocols that serve the organizations well in their normal operations—in part out of legitimate fear that improvisation during a crisis could lead to operational missteps and would, in any event, be almost impossible to coordinate in a system with as many moving, interdependent pieces as in disaster relief. Therefore, as long as one federal agency has responsibility for both business-as-usual disasters with the play-it-by-book procedures (that are propagated on a daily basis to the other elements in the system and reinforced by congressional oversight and political pressures) and catastrophic disasters with a different set of rules, it is likely that the more practiced and familiar by-the-book mindset will leave its mark on the culture and habits of the organization in all circumstances.

Historically, the strategy for overcoming the tyranny of the by-the-book mindset has been the same one that the military uses to prepare its leaders for new situations and exercises. For years FEMA and the states have conducted exercises for catastrophic disasters in which the participants would theoretically be trained in the different rule sets and operating procedures that would come into play. As valuable as these exercises are, it seems clear from the record that they have not done enough to prepare federal, state, and local agencies for the efforts that are required of them in hurricanes such as Katrina and Andrew. It is obviously true that exercises can never replicate the intensity, complexity, or informational uncertainty of a real event. Moreover, they take place too infrequently and, because disaster preparedness is rarely a high priority issue, often involve too few of the key people to really make a difference.

REDESIGNING THE FEDERAL ROLE

The only alternative to continued reliance on the status quo's reliance upon between-catastrophe exercises is to separate the organizational responsibilities for catastrophic and routine disasters. Two ways of accomplishing the separation should be considered. One is to adopt the Canadian or Australian model under which the federal government would essentially shed responsibility for most of the disasters in which it is ordinarily involved.

If the Canadian or Australian model were adopted for routine disasters, presidential disaster declarations would become considerably less frequent as they would be required only when a state requested physical, operational assistance from the federal government. Under such a system, states would spend whatever they choose on relief for a disaster and once that spending reached a preset level, federal reimbursement would become automatically available and the sole federal role would ordinarily be issuing the reimbursement checks according to a predetermined formula, perhaps 50 or 75 percent of the state expenditures over whatever level is set for triggering federal reimbursement. This is, in fact, not so different from what actually happens today for most disasters. For example, all of the first nine disasters declared in 2006 were after-the-fact reimbursements that involved only two steps—making the disaster declarations and issuing reimbursement for eligible state expenditures. Under this approach the states or a contractor hired by the federal government would operate the telephone, banks, and applications centers where disaster victims could file for all forms of assistance from federal and state agencies as well as nongovernmental organizations.

One of the most important benefits of this approach is that it would greatly reduce the number of disasters in which FEMA would be directly involved. This should enable it to concentrate promoting and evaluating preparedness for all emergencies at all levels of the disaster relief system, developing more vigorous training and exercise programs, and providing operational support to states after catastrophic disasters. A second positive effect would be that the states' primary and the federal government's secondary responsibilities for disaster relief would be clarified to the public and the media. As state governments would then become unambiguously responsible for disaster response, this should result in greater political attention to preparedness at the level of state and local governments.

A second approach to redesigning the federal role in disasters would be to establish disaster relief organization in the Executive Office of the

President to oversee federal preparedness activities and provide policy direction to federal operations during a catastrophic disaster. One model that has been proposed repeatedly by the GAO is for a catastrophic disaster unit in the White House. In some respects a catastrophic disaster unit would amount to a partial reestablishment of the Office of Emergency Preparedness that was abolished in the early 1970s as part of an effort to trim down the size of the White House staff. Another option is to designate the FEMA directorship as a dual appointment, the second being as a White House assistant to the president as recommended by the Senate's Committee on Homeland Security and Governmental Affairs, although the Committee believed that FEMA should be abolished and replaced by a new agency that would look very much like FEMA and would remain inside the Department of Homeland Security.[7] Since the White House has had to intervene, sometimes belatedly, after each of the catastrophic disasters covered in this book, establishing a catastrophic disaster unit would not represent a dramatic break with past practice.

However, simply establishing an office in the White House may not make a material difference in the effectiveness of the disaster relief system. In fact, evidence suggests that special-purpose White House units created to bring focus and give direction to multiagency activities are generally toothless and quickly become reduced to the status of bureaucratic window dressing—underfunded and underempowered, but maintained in existence primarily to create the appearance of progress. Various "tsars" have, for example, been appointed with modest effect to coordinate federal operations and policies with respect to AIDS, drug abuse, and even homeland security. However, the real action has always remained with the departments and agencies because they are the ones who possess the manpower, equipment, budget, and authorities and procedures for managing the acquisition and distribution of relief supplies. A small office in the White House can never have any of these capabilities and must therefore depend upon the same agencies that FEMA depends upon. Thus it seems likely that a "disaster tsar" in the White House will ultimately run into the same alignment problem that has affected previous White House tsars and indeed the director of FEMA. That is to say, the appointee would likely have more apparent responsibility than actual power to influence such things as the quality of the preparedness measures undertaken by federal agencies.

It may be that the only way to ensure that preparedness and catastrophic disaster response have sufficient priority is to address the alignment problem directly by resurrecting the stillborn Emergency Management Council of the Carter administration, rather than a mini-Office of Emergency Preparedness, and to assign the responsibility for hands-on oversight of the disaster relief system to the vice president as chair of the Council. A high-level White House council composed of senior officials from the agencies with major responsibilities under the National Response Plan would provide a more effective mechanism for monitoring and appraising agency investments in preparedness.

In any event, greater White House involvement will be essential if the shortcomings of the past are to be avoided in the future. However, if the White House involvement evolves into mere window dressing, in five or ten years—hopefully the next Hurricane Katrina or Andrew will not make landfall sooner—the result will very likely be another operational failure.

COMMUNICATIONS, COMMUNICATIONS, COMMUNICATIONS

Everyone knows the old saw about real estate—that the three most important features about a property are "location, location, and location." Looking over the after-action reports from major disasters and terrorist attacks, it would be fair to make a similar statement about disaster operations—that the three most important features of an operation are "communications, communications, and communications." Indeed the postmortems from the failed relief operations covered in this book provide vivid examples of the problems that result from inadequate or erratic communications. Those problems fall into two categories: lateral communications among the federal agencies and vertical communications from the first responders in the communities most affected by the disaster. Communication problems among the federal agencies are really more a matter of agencies not knowing how the disaster relief system is supposed to work than a hardware shortfall. The vertical communication problem is more a matter of hardware.

As was the case after Hurricane Andrew and, particularly, Hurricane Katrina, many key local government agencies lost their communications for short periods of time due to storm damage and were unable to report on the local situation for a few crucial hours when the state and federal governments were trying to get a handle on where the damage was worst and the needs of disaster victims most acute. The solution to this problem is for the federal government to continue offering preparedness grants that the states can use to purchase more robust and interoperable communications.

Currently these grants are being made available through the Department of Homeland Security. One of the curiosities of the disaster relief program is that FEMA and its predecessor agencies have been issuing grants to state and local governments for improvements in hardware and facilities since the very beginning of the cold war; yet interoperable and survivable communications are still not standard fare at the state and local levels. This is the result of a number of things such as the absence of uniform equipment standards, differences in how quickly new equipment is installed in different jurisdictions, continued reliance upon legacy systems due to familiarity or the delays in new-equipment training, and imperfect business decisions by state and local purchasing agents. Clearly, robust, interoperable communications deserve continued emphasis and more forceful supervision from the federal level.

The issue of federal-level communications is a persistent one, one that has resisted solution in part because the disaster relief system in full array is so highly complex. If there is a single agency in the U.S. government that is relatively good at managing the command and control functions of complex operations, it is the military. Indeed, the military is by far the most conscientious and effective agency in government at exercising the procedures, skills, and mindsets necessary to coordinate complex operations. For this reason, consideration should be given to assigning the military with the mission of developing and managing both a command and control structure for disaster operations and a program for conducting drills and exercises that would work out over time the kinks in command and control procedures, identify gaps in operational plans, and train federal agency personnel.

The military already utilizes the joint task force (JTF) structure in much the same way that the disaster relief community relies upon the Incident Management System—a standardizing approach for organizing the management of disaster operations—and JTFs have been used since at least Hurricane Andrew to manage the military's substantial disaster relief efforts. A standing JTF, in effect a headquarters staff in cadre form that would be supplemented by trained officials, could be established to provide the framework for exercises and drills for catastrophic disasters. Indeed, there already is a standing Joint Task Force-Civil Support for managing military support to the response to terrorist incidents involving chemical, biological, or nuclear terrorism. A standing Joint Task Force-Catastrophic Disaster would provide a more effective structure for resolving command and control issues and identifying holes in operational plans during the preparedness time frame. This Joint Task Force-Catastrophic Disaster could even be administered by the military under contract to the Department of Homeland Security for integration into the Joint Field Office that would be set up by FEMA or a successor agency to manage federal support to states in a catastrophic disaster.

A drawback to reliance upon military command and control mechanisms is the lack of enthusiasm in military circles for additional missions, particularly politically controversial missions that another agency has not always handled well. Moreover, the military is already stretched thin by overseas operations and is facing significant budget pressures of its own. On the other hand, most of the development work for a standing JTF is done by contractors under military supervision and contractors typically design and execute the exercises and drills that enable the JTF structure to function as well as it does. Contractors even manage the process of compiling and evaluating "lessons learned" from previous exercises and real-world operations. There is no reason why such a hybrid, contractor-military model could not be adopted for catastrophic disaster relief.

THE DILEMMA OF SIMPLIFICATION

One of the themes in this book has been that the disaster relief system is too complex for its own good. The system is, in fact, analogous to a closet or cabinet that has been overfilled with pyramided jars, cans, and boxes. Everything works well if the door is opened carefully and the items on the shelves are moved in exactly the right order, so that other jars, cans, and boxes do not fall out. Much the same is true for the disaster relief system, for most disaster conditions are predictable enough for the equivalent of the right jars and cans to be moved without toppling all of the other jars and cans. But if the door is thrown open suddenly and a jar upon which others are balanced falls, the contents of the cabinet will spill onto the floor.

This is ultimately what has happened in the disaster relief system. Before emergencies strike, insufficient attention is paid by everyone to the positioning of the jars on the shelf and their relationships to each other. As a result, during a chaotic relief situation such as those after Hurricanes Andrew and Katrina when key jars and boxes shift, the system fails.

It is, nevertheless, a fact that the disaster relief system is complex for some very basic reasons that are not going to change. There is, first of all, the complexity introduced by the division of responsibilities among the federal, state-local, and private sector elements in the system. Secondly, at each level, responsibilities are dispersed among large numbers of organizations and individuals. Third, most of the federal and state agencies with fingers in the disaster relief pie are themselves composites of subagencies with different organizational capabilities and cultures. Fourth, some of the tasks associated with disaster relief are by their very nature highly complex and require specialized expertise. Examples include search and rescue in collapsed buildings, fire suppression, toxic spill containment, and medical treatment of disaster victims. Moreover, this particular aspect of complexity will certainly grow more daunting as long as the nation is at risk of chemical, biological, and nuclear terrorism. Fifth, there is informational complexity labeled earlier as the "fog" of disaster relief in which there is both temporary uncertainty about exactly what the most important needs are during the first day or two of a relief operation and information overload as more and more data about the disaster begins to flow and all of the federal, state, local, and private sector entities affected by the disaster or participating in the relief effort begin to articulate their observations, needs, capabilities, and priorities.

By and large these complexities are constructive. It hardly makes sense, for example, for a federal disaster relief agency to have all of the response capabilities of the Department of Defense. It is far more economical, and usually just as effective for the disaster relief agency to rely upon the Defense Department to provide manpower, trucks, airlift, and other useful assets when there is a catsatrophic disaster or terrorist event. Nor does it make sense for the federal government to attempt to duplicate the important capabilities that the private sector and state/local governments contribute during disasters.

However, there are conditions under which this finely balanced and interdependent system does not function particularly well, like the overfilled cabinet that has spilled its contents. In response to each of those occasions in which the disaster relief system did not function well (Three Mile Island, Hurricanes Agnes, Hugo, Andrew, and Katrina), what were thought of at the time as "major" reforms were implemented. Obviously, these reforms have failed to accomplish their objectives and the nation is still not in possession of a disaster relief system that is capable of responding quickly and effectively to catastrophic hurricanes and, perhaps, other truly major manmade or natural disasters.

Other reforms have been recommended over the years, but were either not adopted or only partially adopted. The Carter administration's Emergency Management Council and the GAO recommended catsatrophic disaster unit are two examples. As has been noted throughout this book, the preferred policy has however been for presidents to rely upon ad hoc interventions to get the system moving in the right direction. Until Hurricane Katrina, this preference for the ad hoc may have seemed wise given the modest impacts that other single-issue White House offices, such as the various "tsars," have had, although it is equally clear that ad hoc interventions have done little of lasting consequence in terms of boosting the preparedness of the federal departments and agencies.

CONCLUSIONS

The finger-pointing in Washington that occurs after unsuccessful relief operations such as the response to Three Mile Island and Hurricanes Hugo, Andrew, and Katrina has never served a particularly constructive purpose.

It has always left the public with the impression that the problem in the disaster relief system is that key federal officials did not function as effectively as they should have. While it is true that federal performance may have left much to be desired, it does *not* follow that if the key federal officials had done a better job, the relief operations would have succeeded in quickly sheltering, feeding, and rescuing all of the disaster victims. The emphasis on the failings of key individuals has the particularly unfortunate consequence of implying that the problem of poor system performance has a relatively simple solution—appointing more effective executives in the agencies that did not acquit themselves well.

Obviously, it always makes sense to appoint highly capable executives to leadership positions and provide them with the status and power that they need to do their jobs. Nevertheless, there is nothing in the history of the disaster relief system that clearly indicates that a change in the leadership of a single agency will generate a dramatic improvement in the system's performance during catastrophic hurricanes or other major disasters and terrorist incidents. Nor is there convincing evidence that it matters very much whether FEMA or its successor agency is an independent agency or part of a larger department. Too much depends upon the other elements in the complex system for these things to be decisive.

What would make a dramatic difference is the simplification of the system; but herein lies a dilemma. Because there are so many moving pieces, a more simplified response structure than the fifteen working groups and twenty-six agencies that the National Response Plan superimposes upon an almost equally complex structure at the state and local levels may not be realistic. Further the system's complexity is actually a source of efficiency and effectiveness most of the time. The only simplification that may be possible is for the federal government to narrow its focus to disasters in which it will have an operational role and allow reimbursement for other disasters to be handled automatically without requiring a disaster declaration by the president. This would enable the federal government's disaster agency to concentrate more on orchestrating the overall preparedness of the system and on preparing to provide the states operational support during catastrophes. It would also make the states more unambiguously responsible for disaster reliefwhich in itself should lead to improvements in the system's capabilities.

Indeed, another of the lessons from each of the catastrophic disasters of the past is that agencies at all levels need to do more with respect to preparedness. The February 2006 White House report on Hurricane Katrina, for example, lists a startling number of "lessons learned" that essentially conclude that particular agencies should pay more attention to preparedness. Somewhat the same conclusions were drawn by the postmortems after Hurricanes Andrew, Hugo, and Three Mile Island and were also encapsulated in the National Governors Association report of 1978 and President Carter's reorganization plan of 1979. That preparedness has been repeatedly highlighted as a major concern after each operational failure suggests that the problem is systemic and cannot be fully attributed to the characteristics of individual executives or of a single agency. It also suggests that unless a systemic solution is attempted, the next postmortems will conclude that more should have been done now to prepare the system for the next Hurricane Katina.

Preparedness should be a never-ending cycle, akin to walking on a treadmill in that there is no finish line, and there will never be enough money in the budget for everyone to become fully prepared for everything. There will always be new executives and staff to train, new technologies to incorporate, and, unfortunately, new threats to consider. Indeed this is a major reason why a standing JTF should be set up by the military to provide the communications backbone for catastrophic disaster operations and to serve as a vehicle for continuous training and for integrating new communications technologies.

Even if such things as personnel turnover and the introduction of new technologies could be held constant, preparedness must continue to evolve because the environment will change as a result of industrial development, population movement, the construction of new infrastructure, or indeed the deterioration of old infrastructure. Human nature as reinforced by the bureaucratic and political pressures is such, though, that enthusiasm for preparedness always fades between disasters, as more urgent day-to-day operations consume the attention of agency leadership and legislatures. Ad hoc interventions by the president are helpful in that they may temporarily highlight the importance of preparedness, but the reality is that except in the immediate aftermath of a Hurricane Katrina, disaster preparedness is always going to be a secondary or a tertiary priority for every federal agency, that is, except FEMA or its successor agency. But under the current system FEMA is, itself, too absorbed in managing assistance for routine disasters and the practices it follows in managing those disasters seem not to have stood it well during unusually severe disasters.

That is why the responsibility for overseeing federal and system wide preparedness should be taken from FEMA and added to the vice president's portfolio or assigned to an Emergency Management Council based in the White House. The disaster relief system is not a federal government system. It is ultimately a national system, not a federal sysyem and it should thus be overseen by an individual or organization of national stature and should include representatives from the National Governors Association. Congress should contribute to this process by directing the GAO to develop a process for periodically evaluating the the preparedness of the system as a whole, not just the preparedness of the federal agencies.

As we learned in Hurricane Katrina, the administrative fine tuning that was done after Hurricane Agnes, Three Mile Island, and Hurricanes Hugo and Andrew did not result in a system that was capable of responding effectively to catastrophic disasters. There is no reason to believe that another round of fune tuning will make enough of a difference in the future. More basic, structural changes such as the ones outlined in this book need to be made in order for the system to handle the next catastrophic disaster or terrorist event. . . . And the ones after that.

NOTES

CHAPTER 1

1. The FEMA Web site has an archive of disaster declarations. There were three disasters declared in 1994 for *El Nino* effects on the salmon industry, one each for California, Washington, and Oregon; http://www.fema.gov/news/disasters.fema?year=1994.

2. FEMA Web site: http://www.fema.gov/news/newsrelease.fema?id=8030.

3. Committee on Homeland Security and Governmental Affairs, U.S. Senate, *Hurricane Katrina: A Nation Still Unprepared*, April 27, 2006.

4. Mary Murray, "Katrina aid from Cuba? No thanks, says U.S.," *MSNBC.com*, September 4, 2005; http://www.msnbc.msn.com/id/9311876/.

5. The Federal Response Plan lists twenty-seven agencies as signatories and participants. This plan has been incorporated into the National Response Plan of the Department of Homeland Security. The Federal Response Plan is available on the Internet at http://www.fema.gov/rrr/frp/.

6. Hank Christen, Paul Maniscalco, Alan Vickery, and Frances Winslow, "An Overview of the Incident Management System," *Perspectives on Preparedness*, John F. Kennedy School of Government, Harvard University, September 2001, No. 4.

7. Government Accountability Office, Expedited Assistance for Victims of Hurricanes Katrina and Rita: FEMA's Control Weaknesses Exposed the Government to Significant Fraud and Abuse, GAO 06-403T, February 13, 2006.

8. Eric Lipton and Ron Nixon, "Many Contracts for Storm Work Raise Questions," *New York Times*, September 5, 2005; http://www.nytimes.com/2005/09/26/national/nationalspecial/26spend.html?ex=1285387200en=16d1c769d54e8c3c&ei=5088&partner=rssnyt&emc=rss.

9. Greta Wodele, "Committee members irked by Katina contracting practices," *Government Executive*, Daily Briefing, November 3, 2005 (http://www.govexec.com/dailyfed/1105/110305cdam2.htm); Ana Radelat, "Louisiana businesses get only small FEMA contracts," *The Shreveport Times*, November 25, 2005 (http://www.shreveporttimes.com/apps/pbcs.dll/article?AID=/20051125/NEWS01/511250304/1002/NEWS). Similar stories were aired on television and radio news in early November, 2005. For example, CBS television on November 11, 2005 (http://www.cbsnews.com/stories/2005/11/11/national/main1041326.shtml).

10. Gaines Foster, *The Demands of Humanity: Army Medical Disaster Relief* (Washington, DC: Center for Military History, 1983), p. 78.

11. The National Response Plan is available on the Department of Homeland Security Web site at http://www.dhs.gov/interweb/assetlibrary/NRPbaseplan.pdf.

12. A copy of the 1987 earthquake plan is available at the following Web site: http://cidbimena.desastres.hn/docum/crid/Julio-Agosto2005/CD2/pdf/eng/doc1816/doc1816.htm.

13. Some examples of newspaper articles in which former FEMA officials condemned the agency's merger into the Department of Homeland Security are as follows: Peter G. Gosselin and Alan C. Miller, "Why FEMA Was Missing in Action," *Los Angeles Times*, September 5, 2005 (http://www.latimes.com/news/nationworld/nation/la-na-fema5sep05,0,2650635,full.story?coll=la-home-headlines); Public Broadcasting Service, "Now," September 30, 2005 (http://www.pbs.org/now/transcript/transcriptNOW139_full.html); CBS News, "Special Report—In Katrina's Wake: The Blame Game," September 7, 2005 (http://www.cbsnews.com/stories/2005/09/07/katrina/main821705.shtml).

14. Christiansen, Maniscalco, Vickery, and Winslow, *Perspectives on Preparedness*, p. 2.

15. Dana Cole, *The Incident Command System: A 25-year Evaluation by California Practitioners*, February 2000, p. 9; http://www.usfa.fema.gov/pdf/efop/efo31023.pdf.

16. Donna Brown, "A Tale of Two Cities," *Management Review*, 79(2), February 1990, 50–54.

CHAPTER 2

1. United States Geological Survey, "Earthquake Facts and Lists: The Modified Mercalli Intensity Scale," http://neic.usgs.gov/neis/general/mercalli.html.

2. National Climatic Data Center, National Oceanographic and Atmospheric Administration, "Billion Dollar U.S. Weather Disasters," http://www.ncdc.noaa.gov/oa/reports/billionz.html#chron.

3. The United States Geological Survey Cascades Volcano Observatory has extensive information about the 1980 eruption and subsequent volcanic activity at Mt St Helens at its Web site http://vulcan.wr.usgs.gov/.

4. Rutherford H. Platt, *Disasters and Democracy: The Politics of Extreme Natural Events* (Washington, DC: Island Press, 1999), p. 249.

5. Washington Post/Kaiser Family Foundation/Harvard University, *Survey of Hurricane Katrina Evacuees*, September 2005, pp. 4 and 13; http://www.kff.org/newsmedia/upload/7401.pdf.

6. Greater New Orleans Community Data Center, "Reported Locations of Katrina/Rita Applicants" October 31, 2005; http://www.gnocdc.org/maps/PDFs/Katrina_Rita_appl.doc.

7. "USA Today/CNN/Gallup Poll," October 14, 2005; http://www.usatoday.com/news/polls/2005-10-14-redcross-poll.htm.

8. John R. Logan, National Science Foundation, January 26, 2006.

9. U.S. Census Bureau, "Fact Sheet: New Orleans City, Louisiana," 2000; http://factfinder.census.gov/servlet/SAFFFacts?_event=Search&geo_id=&_geoContext=&_street=&_county=New±Orleans&_cityTown=New±Orleans&_state=04000US22&_zip=&_lang=en&_sse=on&pctxt=fph&pgsl=010.

10. Arian Campo-Flores, "A New Spice in the Gumbo," Newsweek, December 5, 2005; http://msnbc.msn.com/id/10218343/site/newsweek/.

11. U.S. Hispanic Chamber of Commerce, "USHCC Deplores Remarks by New Orleans Mayor Ray Nagin Regarding Mexican Workers and the Rebuilding of New Orleans," Press Release, October 28, 2005; http://www.hispanicbusiness.com/news/newsbyid.asp?id=26340.

12. James Varney, "Nuevo Orleans?" *The Times-Picayune*, October 18, 2005 (http://www.nola.com/news/t-p/frontpage/index.ssf?/base/news-4/1129615103205800.xml); Jonathan Tilove, "Cleanup relies upon day labor of Latinos," *The Times-Picayune*, January 8, 2006 (http://nola.live.advance.net/news/t-p/frontpage/index.ssf?/base/news-4/113670629389340.xml).

13. Census Bureau, op cit.

14. A copy of the Stafford Act is at the FEMA Web site http://www.fema.gov/library/stafact.shtm#sec102.

CHAPTER 3

1. Jeorge R. Beler, "The Philippine Army in Disaster Relief Operations," *Army Trooper Newsmagazine* (Philippines), January 2003, XVII(1).

2. The list of floods was taken from the U.S. Fifth Army Web site, "Military Support to Civil Authorities (MSCA)," Document undated, accessed May 9, 2006. http://www.5tharmy.army.mil/FifthArmy/about/MSCA.htm.

3. The U.S. Geological Survey, "Casualties and Damage after the 1906 Earthquake," at the USGS Web site http://quake.wr.usgs.gov/info/1906/casualties.html. An extensive collection of photographs from the earthquake is available on the Internet—many of the sites for these collections are linked to the U.S. Geological Survey site: http://quake.wr.usgs.gov/info/1906/photos.html.

4. The Brookings Institution, "Timeline of Military Deployments for Katrina Disaster Relief," http://www.brookings.edu/fp/projects/homeland/katrinamilitarydeployments.pdf.

5. General Accounting Office (now Government Accountability Office), *Disaster Assistance: DOD's Support for Hurricanes Andrew and Iniki and Typhoon Omar*, (NSIAD-93-180), June 1993, p. 2.

6. Department of Homeland Security, *National Response Plan*, December 2004, p. 62

7. Julia Duchovny, "St Petersburg Holiday Shoppers Face Gas Attack," *Moscow News*, December 30, 2005, no. 50, 2005. http://english.mn.ru/english/issue.php? 2005–50-6. "Gas Poisons Russian shoppers," Cable News Network, December 26, 2005. http://www.cnn.com/2005/WORLD/asiapcf/12/26/russia.gas.ap/?section= cnn_world.

8. U.S. Government, War Department, *Special Regulation No.67; Regulations Governing Flood Relief Work of the War Department*, (Washington: U.S. Government Printing Office, 1917), U.S. National Archives, Record Group Number 407.

9. Hank Christen, Paul Maniscalco, Alan Vickery, Frances Winslow, "An Overview of the Incident Management System," *Perspectives on Preparedness*, September 2001, No. 4. Harvard University, John F. Kennedy School of Government.

10. U.S. Department of Justice, Press Release: "Attorney General Alberto Gonzales Outlines Anti-Fraud Priorities to Protect the Integrity of Relief Efforts in Hurricane Katrina-Stricken Region," September 8, 2005; http://www.usdoj.gov/ opa/pr/2005/September/05_ag_462.htm.

11. Indictments are listed at the FBI Web site, "Hurricane Katrina/Rita Information," http://www.fbi.gov/katrina.htm.

12. Government Accountability Office, *Expedited Assistance for Victims of Hurricanes Katrina and Rita*, GAO-06-403T, February 13, 2006, p. 1.

13. Gaines Foster, *The Demands of Humanity: Army Medical Disaster Relief* (Washington, DC: Center for Military History, 1983), p. 78.

14. Ted Steinberg, *Acts of God: The Unnatural History of Natural Disaster in America* (New York: Oxford University Press, 2000), pp. 17–18.

15. Northwestern University and the Chicago Historical Society, "The Great Chicago Fire," October 8, 1996; http://www.chicagohistory.org/fire/conflag/ pic0029.html.

16. A copy of the order is available at the online exhibition of the San Francisco Museum, http://www.sfmuseum.org/1906.2/killproc.html.

17. A copy of the Secretary of War's guidance is available at the online exhibition of the San Francisco Museum, http://www.sfmuseum.org/1906/conflict.html.

18. Jennifer Elsea, *The Use of Federal Troops for Disaster Assistance: Legal Issues* Congressional Research Service, (Report No. RS 22266), September 16, 2005, p. 3.

19. Ibid., p. 3.

20. US Northern Command homepage http://www.northcom.mil/index.cfm? fuseaction=s.who_mission.

CHAPTER 4

1. "Disasters: The Violent Deadly Swath of Agnes," *Time*, July 3, 1972, p. 9.

2. "Disasters: Agnes," *Newsweek*, July 3, 1972, p. 15.

3. "Disasters: The Violent Deadly Swath of Agnes," *Time*, July 3, 1972, p. 9.

4. Richard Sanderson of the OEP is quoted in Mioichael T. Kaufman, "Vignettes of Tragedy—and Quiet Courage," *The New York Times*, June 28, 1972, p. 5.

5. Robert Belingfield, "Erie Road, Citing Flood, Files for Reorganization," *The New York Times*, June 27, 1972, p. 1.

6. Nancy Scannell, "Congress Passes Emergency Flood Relief," *The Washington Post*, July 1, 1972, p. A1.

7. Paul L. Montgomery, "Flood Areas Rally as Waters Recede," *The New York Times*, June 26, 1972, p. 1.

8. "Washington: For the Record," *The Washington Post*, June 26, 1972, p. 16.

9. "Washington: For the Record," *The Washington Post*, June 29, 1972, p. 18.

10. Press Secretary Ronald Ziegler is quoted in Michael Knight, "Nixon Asks $100 Million in Flood Relief," *The New York Times*, June 28, 1972, p. 28.

11. "Holiday Is Used Upstate to Clean Up After Flood," *The New York Times*, July 3, 1972, p. 32.

12. Nancy Scannell, "Housing Remains Acute Problem: For 10,000, Flood Is Still Real," The Washington Post, July 5, 1972, p. A1.

13. General Accounting Office (renamed in 2004 the Government Accountability Office), *Administrative Problems Experienced in Providing Federal Assistance to Disaster Victims*, November 15, 1973, p. 2.

14. General Accounting Office, Letter Report to the Secretary of Housing and Urban Development, December 31, 1975.

15. Nuclear Regulatory Commission, "Fact Sheet on the Accident at Three Mile Island," March 2004; http://www.nrc.gov/reading-rm/doc-collections/fact-sheets/3mile-isle.html.

16. For example, Andrew Hopkins, "Was Three Mile Island a 'Normal Accident'?" *Journal of Contingencies and Crisis Management*, June 2001, 9(2), 65–72.

17. President's Commission, *Report of the President's Commission on the Accident at Three Mile Island* (Washington, DC: Government Printing Office, October 1979), p. 17.

18. Oran K. Henderson, "Commonwealth of Pennsylvania Emergency Preparedness and Response: The Three Mile Island Incident," in Thomas H. Moss and David L. Sills (eds.), *The Three Mile Island Nuclear Accident: Lessons and Implications* (New York: New York Academy of Sciences, 1981), pp. 317–318.

19. President's Commission, *Report of the President's Commission on the Accident at Three Mile Island*, p. 39.

20. J. Samuel Walker, *Three Mile Island: A Nuclear Crisis in Historical Perspective* (Los Angeles: University of California Press, 2004), p. 126.

21. Ibid., p 57.

22. Ibid., pp. 134, 159–62.

23. The text of the Cronkite statement is quoted in David M. Rubin, "What the President's Commission Learned About the Media," in Thomas H. Moss and David L. Sills (eds.), *The Three Mile Island Nuclear Accident: Lessons and Implications* (New York: New York Academy of Sciences, 1981), pp. 98–99.

24. President's Commission, *Report of the President's Commission on the Accident at Three Mile Island*, p. 58.

25. Walker, *Three Mile Island: A Nuclear Crisis in Historical Perspective*, p. 102; Rubin, "What the President's Commission Learned About the Media," pp. 101–102.

26. National Governors Association, *1978 Emergency Preparedness Project: Final Report* (Washington, DC: National Governors Association, 1979), pp. xi–xiii.

27. National Academy of Public Administration, *Coping With Catastrophe: Building an Emergency Management System to Meet Peoples' Needs in Natural and Manmade Disasters* (Washington, DC, February 1993), p. 14.

28. National Governors Association, *1978 Emergency Preparedness Project*, pp. xiii–xiv.

CHAPTER 5

1. Senator Hollings' words have been variously quoted as the "biggest bunch" and the "sorriest bunch" Michael Vines, "Congress Votes Sharp Increase in Storm Relief," *The New York Times*, September 29, 1989, p. A1.

2. Quoted in a *St. Petersburg Times* retrospective on the ten-year anniversary of Hurricane Andrew, Bill Addair, "10 years ago, her angry plea got hurricane aid moving," *St. Petersburg Times*, August 20, 2002. The first part of the quote was widely reported at the time and has since been cited with reference to Hurricane Katrina.

3. Tom Matthews, "What Went Wrong," *Newsweek*, September 7, 1992, p. 23.

4. Anon., "Hugo: A Case Study," *UN Chronicle*, June 1991, 28(2), 50.

5. Testimony of John M. Otis of the General Accounting Office, "Disaster Assistance: Federal, State and Local Responses to Natural Disasters Need Improvement," Released May 15, 1991 (GAO/T-RCED-91–39), p. 1.

6. General Accounting Office, *Disaster Assistance: Federal, State and Local Responses to Natural Disasters Need Improvement*, (GAO/ RCED 91–43) March 1991, p. 20.

7. National Oceanographic and Atmospheric Administration, *Billion Dollar U.S. Weather Disasters*, September 9, 2005; http://www.ncdc.noaa.gov/oa/reports/billionz.html#narrative.

8. Dennis Hevesi, "Full Force of Storm Hits South Carlina," *The New York Times*, September 22, p. A1.

9. Ed Magnuson, "Winds of Chaos," *Time*, October 9, 1989, p. 18.

10. Vines, op cit., p. A14.

11. Ronald Smothers, "Heavy Rains Delay the Vast Cleanup in the South," *The New York Times*, September 26, 1982, p. A1.

12. Ronald Smothers, "Charleston Rushes to Preserve Heritage from Waters," *The New York Times*, September 25, 1982, p. A14.

13. James M. Baker and Howard Manly, "The Storm after Hugo: Did Bush Do Enough?" *Newsweek*, October 9, 1982, p. 40.

14. William L. Waugh and Richard T. Sylves, "The Intergovernmental Relations of Emergency Management," in Waugh and Sylves (eds.), *Disaster Management in the U.S. and Canada: The Politics, Policymaking, Administration and Analysis of Emergency Management*, 2nd edn. (Springfield, IL: Charles C. Thomas Publisher, 1996), p. 50.

15. General Accounting Office, (GAO/ RCED 91-43) March 1991, pp. 43–44.

16. Ibid., p. 43.

17. National Oceanographic and Atmospheric Administration, Billion Dollar U.S. Weather Disasters.

18. General Accounting Office, *Disaster Management: Improving the Nation's Response to Catastrophic Disasters* (Letter report July 23, 1993 GAO/RCED 93-186), p. 1.

19. General Accounting Office, *Disaster Assistance: DOD's Support for Hurricanes Andrew and Iniki and Typhoon Omar* (GAO/NSIAD 93-180), June 1993, p. 21.

20. Mr. Card's biography is at the White House Web site http://www.whitehouse.gov/government/card-bio.html.

21. General Accounting Office, *Disaster Management: Improving the Nation's Response to Catastrophic Disasters* (Letter report July 23, 1993 GAO/RCED 93-186), pp. 1 and 5.

22. General Accounting Office, *Disaster Assistance: DOD's Support for Hurricanes Andrew and Iniki and Typhoon Omar*, p. 15.

23. Ibid., p. 22.

24. The letter is quoted in National Academy of Public Administration, *Coping with Catastrophe: Building an Emergency Management System to in Natural and Manmade Disasters* (Washington, DC: National Academy of Public Administration, February 1993), pp. 1–2.

25. General Accounting Office, *Disaster Management: Improving the Nation's Response to Catastrophic Disasters*, p. 1. Also, *Disaster Assistance: DOD's Support for Hurricanes Andrew and Iniki and Typhoon Omar*, p. 3.

26. National Academy of Public Administration, *Coping with Catastrophe*, pp. xv and 29.

27. Ibid., p. 2.

28. Ibid., p. xx.

29. Ibid., p. xv.

30. General Accounting Office, *GAO Work on Disaster Assistance*, Letter Report GAO/RCED 94–239R, August 31, 1994, pp. 6–7.

31. General Accounting Office, *Disaster Assistance: DOD's Support for Hurricanes Andrew and Iniki and Typhoon Omar*, p. 8.

32. The 1994 reorganization of FEMA, "New Directions and Opportunities" is described at www.fema.gov/rrr/section2.shtm.

33. R. Stephen Daniels and Carolyn Clark-Daniels, *Transforming Government: The Renewal and Revitalization of the Federal Emergency Management Agency*, The PriceWaterhouseCoopers Endowment for the Business of Government,

April 2000, p. 13. This report is sprinkled with effusive praise for Director Witt and the Clinton administration, as well as advice that the second Bush administration did not take. Oddly it was still posted on the FEMA Web site as recently as December 2005—six years after the second administration took office.

CHAPTER 6

1. FEMA Press Release 1603–337, "FEMA Short-Term Lodging: A Transition to Long Term Solutions," February 10, 2006; http://www.fema.gov/news/newsrelease.fema?id=23479. Also FEMA Press Release 1603–344, "Louisiana Weekly Housing Update: FEMA transitions from emergency sheltering to long-term housing assistance," February 13, 2006, http://www.fema.gov/news/newsrelease.fema?id=23619.

2. U.S. Congress, House of Representatives, Select Bipartisan Committee to Investigate the Preparations for and Response to Hurricane Katrina, *A Failure of Initiative: The Final Report of the Select Bipartisan Committee to Investigate the Preparations for and Response to Hurricane Katrina*, (Washington, DC: U.S. Government Printing Office, 2006), February 15, 2006, p. 64.

3. Ibid., p. 344.

4. Douglas Brinkley, *The Great Deluge: Hurricane Katrina, New Orleans, and the Mississippi Gulf Coast* (New York: William Morrow, 2006), pp. 91–92.

5. Ibid., p. 632.

6. Ibid., p. 631.

7. *CNN Reports: Katrina—State of Emergency* (Kansas City: Andrews McNeel Publishing, 2005) [A compilation of CNN reportage], p. 33.

8. Associated Press, "Cops: Superdome Violence Reports Exaggerated," September 27, 2005; http://www.foxnews.com/story/0,2933,170569,00.html. Brian Thevenot and Gordon Russell, "Reports of anarchy at Superdome Overstated," *The Seattle Times*, September 26, 2005; http://seattletimes.nwsource.com/html/nationworld/2002520986_katmyth26.html.

9. Brinkley, *The Great Deluge*, p. 601.

10. Government Accountability Office, *Preliminary Observations Regarding Preparedness and Response to Hurricanes Katrina and Rita* (GAO 06-365R), February 1, 2006, p. 2. This report is the source of the 1.4 million figure. The 1.7 million figure is from the FEMA Web site http://www.fema.gov/press/2005/resources_katrina.shtm. The FEMA figure is as of February 8, 2006.

11. The White House, *The Federal Response to Hurricane Katrina: Lessons Learned*, February 23, 2006, p. 7.

12. Select Bipartisan Committee, *A Failure of Initiative* . . . , p. 201.

13. Steve Bowman, Lawrence Kapp, and Amy Belasco, *CRS Report for Congress: Hurricane Katrina, DOD Disaster Response*, Congressional Research Service, September 19, 2005, p. 11.

14. Select Bipartisan Committee, *A Failure of Initiative* . . . , p. 213.

15. Ibid., p. 346.

16. Ibid., p. 353.

17. American Red Cross, *In the News: Kitchen 44 Closes, Feeding Operations Continue*, February 15, 2006; http://www.redcross.org/article/0,1072,0_276_5107,00.htm.

18. The Center on Philanthropy at Indiana University, *Gulf Coast Hurricane Relief Donations*, January 28, 2006; http://www.philanthropy.iupui.edu/Hurricane_Katrina.html.

19. Entergy Corporation, "Entergy's Power of Hope Fund Stands at $2.9 Million; Power Restored to 860,000 Customers," September 11, 2005; http://www.prnewswire.com/cgi-bin/stories.pl?ACCT=109&STORY=/www/story/09–16–2005/0004109133&EDATE.

20. The White House, *The Federal Response to Hurricane Katrina: Lessons Learned*, p. 8.

21. Congressional Budget Office, *The Macroeconomic and Budgetary Effects of Hurricanes Katrina and Rita: An Update* (Washington, DC: Congressional Budget Office, September 29, 2005), pp. 1–5.

22. Dan Baum, "Deluged: When Katrina Hit, Where Were the Police?" *New Yorker*, January 9, 2006, p. 55.

23. Congressional Budget Office, *The Macroeconomic and Budgetary Effects of Hurricanes Katrina and Rita: An Update*, p. 16.

24. Department of Homeland Security, *National Response Plan*, December 2004, p. 67.

25. Ibid., p. 63.

26. The number of trailer trucks was derived from a chart in The White House, *The Federal Response to Hurricane Katrina: Lessons Learned*, p. 30.

27. Brinkley, *The Great Deluge*, p. 38.

28. Department of Homeland Security, *National Response Plan*, p. 7.

29. The White House, *The Federal Response to Hurricane Katrina: Lessons Learned*, p. 36.

30. Mark Hosenball, "The Back-Channel Chatter After Katrina," *Newsweek*, February 27, 2006, p. 38.

CHAPTER 7

1. Emergency Management Australia, *This Is EMA* (Canberra: Attorney-General's Department, 2005), p. 2.

2. Department of Transport and Regional Services, "Natural Disaster Relief: Natural Disaster Relief Arrangements," August 12, 2005; http://www.dotars.gov.au/localgovt/ndr/arrangements.aspx.

3. FEMA Press Release 1604–249, "Mississippi Recovery Update for Hurricane Katrina: Week 24," February 17, 2006; http://www.fema.gov/news/newsrelease.fema?id=23719.

4. Public Safety and Emergency Preparedness Canada, "Disaster Financial Assistance Arrangements," http://www.psepc-sppcc.gc.ca/prg/em/dfaa/index-en.asp.

5. Centre for Emergency Preparedness and Response, "Two scenarios offer examples if how the centre delivers results for Canadians" Health Canada Web site http://www.phac-aspc.gc.ca/cepr-cmiu/scenario_e.html.

6. Department of National Defence, "Operation Recuperation," http://www.forces.gc.ca/site/operations/recuperation_e.asp.

7. FEMA, "A Guide to the Disaster Declaration Process," http://www.fema.gov/pdf/rrr/dec_proc.pdf, October 23, 2004.

CHAPTER 8

1. The legislation is P.L. 104–321. One of the places where the text is available is the Government Printing Office Web site http://frwebgate.access.gpo.gov/cgi-bin/getdoc.cgi?dbname=104_cong_public_laws&docid=f:publ321.104.pdf.

2. The White House paper is quoted in Rutherford H. Platt, *Disasters and Democracy: The Politics of Extreme Natural Events* (Washington, DC: Island Press, 1999), p. 38. The summary of the House Bipartisan Task Force report is on p. 39.

3. FEMA Press Release 1603-328, "By The Numbers: FEMA Recovery Update in Louisiana," February 1, 2006; http://www.fema.gov/news/newsrelease.fema?id=23178.

4. U.S. Congress, Senate, Committee on Homeland Security and Governmental Affairs, *Hurricane Katrina: A Nation Still Unprepared* (Washington, DC: U.S Senate, May 2006), p. 18.

5. Government Accountability Office, *Disaster Management: Improving the Nation's Response to Catastrophic Disasters* (GAO-RCED 93-186), July 1993, p. 1.

6. Government Accountability Office, *Preliminary Observations on Hurricane Response* (GAO 06-365R), February 1, 2006, p. 4.

7. Committee on Homeland Security and Governmental Affairs, *Hurricane Katrina*, p. 18.

SELECTED RESOURCES

BOOKS AND MAJOR REPORTS

Brinkley, Douglas. *The Great Deluge: Hurricane Katrina, New Orleans, and the Mississippi Gulf Coast* (New York: William Morrow, 2006).

Cutter, Susan L., ed. *American Hazardscapes: The Regionalization of Hazards and Disaster* (Washington, DC: Joseph Henry Press, 2001).

Daniels, R. Stephen and Clark-Daniels, Carolyn L. *Transforming Government: The Renewal and Revitalization of the Federal Emergency Management Agency*, PricewaterhouseCoopers Endowment for Better Government, April 2000.

Department of Homeland Security. *National Response Plan*, December 2004.

Foster, Gaines. *The Demands of Humanity: Army Medical Disaster Relief* (Washington, DC: Center for Military History, 1983).

Mileti, Dennis S., ed. *Disasters by Design: A Reassessment of Natural Hazards in the United States* (Washington, DC: National Academy Press, 1999).

Moss, Thomas H. and Sills, David L., eds. *The Three Mile Island Nuclear Accident: Lessons and Implications* (New York: New York Academy of Sciences, 1981).

National Academy of Public Administration. *Coping with Catastrophe: Building and Emergency Management System That Meets People's Needs in Natural and Manmade Disasters*, February 1993.

National Academy of Public Administration. *Review of Actions Taken to Strengthen the Nation's Emergency Management System: A Study for the Federal Emergency Management Agency*, March 1994.

National Governors Association. *1978 Emergency Preparedness Project: Final Report*, December 31, 1978.

National Science and Technology Council, Working Group on Natural Disaster Information Systems. *Effective Disaster Warnings*, November 2000.

Platt, Rutherford H. *Disasters and Democracy: The Politics of Extreme Natural Events* (Washington, DC: Island Press, 1999).

President's Commission. *Report of the President's Commission on the Accident at Three Mile Island* (Washington, DC: Government Printing Office, October 1979).

Select Bipartisan Committee to Investigate the Preparation for and Response to Hurricane Katrina, U.S. House of Representatives. *A Failure of Initiative: Final Report of the Select Bipartisan Committee to Investigate the Preparation for and Response to Hurricane Katrina* (Washington, DC: Government Printing Office, 2006).

Steinberg, Ted. *Acts of God: The Unnatural History of Natural Disaster in America* (New York: Oxford University Press, 2000).

Townsend, Frances (Assistant to the President for Homeland Security and Counterterrorism). *The Federal Response to Hurricane Katrina: Lessons Learned*, The White House, February 2006.

Walker, J. Samuel. *Three Mile Island: A Nuclear Crisis in Historical Perspective* (Los Angeles: University of California Press, 2004).

Waugh, William L. and Sylves, Richard T., eds. *Disaster Management in the U.S. and Canada: The Politics, Policymaking, Administration and Analysis of Emergency Management*, 2nd edn. (Springfield, IL: Charles C. Thomas Publisher, 1996).

ARTICLES, PAPERS, AND REPORTS

Bazan, Elizabeth B. *Robert T. Stafford Disaster Relief and Emergency Assistance Act: Legal Requirements for Federal and State Roles in Declarations of an Emergency or a Major Disaster*, Congressional Research Service, RL33090, September 16, 2005.

Bea, Keith. *Disaster Evacuation and Displacement Policy: Issues for Congress*, Congressional Research Service, RS22235, September 2, 2005.

———. *FEMA's Mission: Policy Directives for the Federal Emergency Management Agency*, Congressional Research Service, RL31285, March 13, 2002.

———. *FEMA and Disaster Relief*, Congressional Research Service, 97-195 GOV, March 6, 1998.

Bowman, Steve, Kapp, Lawrence, and Belasco, Amy. *Hurricane Katrina: DOD Disaster Response*, Congressional Research Service, RL33095, September 19, 2005.

Canada, Ben. *Recovery from Terrorist Attack: A Catalog of Selected Federal Assistance Programs*, Congressional Research Service, RL31125, February 1, 2002.

Carter, Nicole. *Flood Risk Management: Federal Role in Infrastructure*, Congressional Research Service, RL33129, October 26, 2005.

Christen, Hank, Maniscalco, Paul, Vickery, Alan, and Winslow, Frances. *Perspectives on Preparedness: An Overview of Incident Management Systems*, John F. Kennedy School of Government, September 2001, No. 4.

Comerio, Mary C. "Housing Issues after Disasters," *Journal of Contingencies and Crisis Management*, September 1997, 5(3), 166–178.

Elsea, Jennifer. *The Use of Federal Troops for Disaster Assistance: Legal Issues*, Congressional Research Service, RS22266, September 16, 2005.

General Accounting Office. *Disaster Management: Improving the Nation's Response to Catastrophic Disasters*, GAO/RCED-93-186, July 1993.

———. *Disaster Assistance: DOD's Support for Hurricanes Andrew and Iniki and Typhoon Omar*, GAO/NSIAD-93-180, July 1993.

———. *Disaster Assistance: Supplemental Information on Hurricane Hugo in South Carolina*, GAO/RCED-91-150, May 1991.

———. *Disaster Assistance: Federal, State, and Local Responses to Natural Disasters Need Improvement*, GAO/RCED-91-43, March 1991.

———. *Further Actions Needed to Improve Emergency Preparedness around Nuclear Plants*, GAO/RCED-84-43, August 1, 1984.

———. *Emergency Preparedness around Nuclear Facilities*, Testimony before Congress by Ralph Carlone, Deputy Director Resources, Community and Economic Development, GAO, August 2, 1983.

———. *Emergency Preparedness around Nuclear Facilities*, Testimony before Congress by Dexter Peach, Director of Energy and Minerals Division, GAO, May 16, 1979.

———. *Administrative Problems Experienced in Providing Federal Assistance to Disaster Victims*, B-167790, November 1973.

Government Accountability Office. *Federal Emergency Management Agency: Factors for Future Success and Issues to Consider for Organizational Placement*, GAO-06-746T, May 9, 2006.

———. *Expedited Assistance for Victims of Hurricanes Katrina and Rita: FEMA's Control Weaknesses Exposed the Government to Significant Fraud and Abuse*, GAO-06-403T, February 13, 2006.

———. *Statement by Comptroller General David M. Walker on GAO's Preliminary Observations Regarding Preparedness and Response to Hurricanes Katrina and Rita*, GAO-06-365R, February 1, 2006.

———. *Hurricane Katrina: Providing Oversight of the Nation's Preparedness, Response, and Recovery Activities*, GAO-05-1053T, September 28, 2005.

———. *Disaster Assistance: Improvement Needed in Disaster Declaration Criteria and Eligibility Assurance Procedures*, GAO-01-837, August 2001.

Hogue, Henry B. *Federal Hurricane Recovery Coordinator: Appointment and Oversight Issues*, Congressional Research Service, RS22334, November 28, 2005.

Hogue, Henry B. and Bea, Kenneth. *Federal Emergency Management and Homeland Security Organization: Historical Developments and Legislative Options*, Congressional Research Service, April 19, 2006.

King, Rawle. *Hurricanes and Disaster Risk Financing through Insurance: Challenges and Policy Options*, Congressional Research Service, RL32825, March 25, 2005.

Litan, Robert E. *Preparing for Future "Katrinas,"* The Brookings Institution Policy Brief #150, March 2006.

Metropolitan Policy Program. *New Orleans after the Storm: Lessons from the Past, A Plan for the Future*, The Brookings Institution, October 2005.

Morrow, Betty Hearn. "Identifying and Mapping Community Vulnerability," *Disasters*, 1999, 23(1), 1–18.

Richardson, Joe. *Federal Food Assistance in Disasters: Hurricanes Katrina and Rita*, Congressional Research Service, RL33102, September 23, 2005.

Roberts, Patrick S. "Reputation and Federal Preparedness Agencies, 1948–2003," paper presented at *2004 Annual Meeting of the American Political Science Association*, September 2–4, 2004.

Senate Committee on Homeland Security and Governmental Affairs. *Hurricane Katrina: A Nation Still Unprepared* (Washington, DC, May 2006).

Sylves, Richard T. "Ferment at FEMA: Reforming Emergency Management," *Public Administration Review*, May/June 1994, 303–307.

WEB SITES

Cascades Volcano Observatory, http://vulcan.wr.usgs.gov/.

Chicago Historical Society, http://www.chicagohistory.org/fire/.

Department of Homeland Security, http://www.dhs.gov/dhspublic/.

Emergency Management Australia, http://www.ema.gov.au.

Federal Emergency Management Agency, http://www.fema.gov.

National Climatic Data Center, http://www.ncdc.noaa.gov/oa/reports/billionz.html.

National Earthquake Information Center, http://neic.usgs.gov.

National Emergency Management Association, http://www.nemaweb.org/.

National Hurricane Center, http://www.nhc.noaa.gov/.

Natural Hazards Center, http://www.colorado.edu/hazards/.

Nuclear Regulatory Commission, http://www.nrc.gov.

Public Safety and Emergency Preparedness, Canada, http://www.psepc-sppcc.gc.ca/.

Red Cross, http://www.redrcoss.org.

San Francisco Museum, http://www.sfmuseum.org/1906.

State Emergency Management Agency's link, http://www.fema.gov/fema/statedr.shtm.

United States Geological Survey, http://neic.usgs.gov.

United States Northern Command, http://www.northcom.mil.

INDEX

About the Author

JAMES F. MISKEL is a consultant for the defense consulting firm Alidade Inc. Until 2005, he served for 12 years as Professor of National Security Affairs at the Naval War College, where he still teaches online courses in the graduate degree program. During the Reagan and (first) Bush Administration he served on the National Security Council.